DATE DUE

DEC 1 5 2001			

Demco No. 62-0549

JS
1228
K58
1991

A citizen's guide to how city government works

What makes New York City run?

by

Adrienne Kivelson

published by

The League of Women Voters of the City of New York Education Fund
817 Broadway, New York, New York 10003-4760

This publication was made possible, in part, by grants from
Charles H. Revson Foundation
The New York Times Company Foundation

©1991, Revised Edition by
The League of Women Voters of the City of New York
817 Broadway, New York, New York 10003-4760

Illustrations ©1979 by Jeff Seaver
Design by Bill Hine

All rights reserved
Library of Congress Catalogue Card Number   91-061162
ISBN 0-916130-02-9

Printed on recycled paper in the United States of America
99 98 97 96 95 94 93   5 4 3 2 1

Just as New Yorkers need subway and road maps to get around the five boroughs—they need a guide to navigate New York City government.

Adrienne Kivelson, who wrote the first *What makes New York City run?* in 1979, took on the year-long task of deciphering the 330-page New York City Charter, reviewing innumerable city reports, researching and writing the 1991 edition. She not only had to take into account the charter revisions approved by the voters in the 1989 election, but if, when and how these changes are being implemented.

The League of Women Voters of the City of New York is pleased to present this guide in the belief that every citizen should be able to participate intelligently in the decision-making process of government.

Special thanks are extended to Lenore Chester, associate director of Citizens Union Foundation and a past president of the League of Women Voters of the City of New York for her tireless research efforts and invaluable suggestions; and to Eric Lane, professor of law at the School of Law, Hofstra University, who served as chair of the Mayor's Task Force on Charter Implementation, and executive director of the Charter Revision Commission, for reading the manuscript and offering constructive recommendations, and to Patricia Young who edited and expedited this work.

Because New York City is constantly changing—New Yorkers need to understand what makes New York City run—we hope that this citizen's guide will serve that purpose.

Laura Altschuler, President   May 1991

Table of Contents

Introduction	9
New York City– not an island unto itself	15
What makes New York City run? the Charter	19
Who makes New York City run?	23
The Mayor	23
The President of the City Council	27
The Comptroller	29
The Borough Presidents	32
The City Council	34
The Districting Commission	38
The Community Boards	40
How New York City plans its spending– the budgets	45
Who pays for New York City government?	53
How contracts are awarded	57
Land Use and City Planning	61
Open and Participatory Government	73
Conflicts of Interest	74
Public Hearings	77
City Agencies	79
Conclusion	97

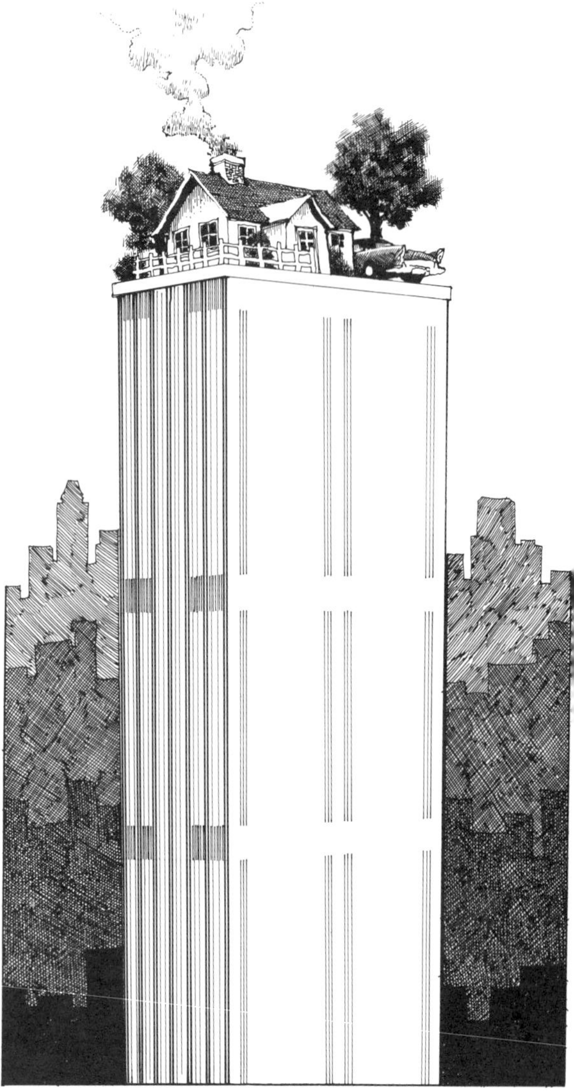

Introduction

What makes New York City run? was first published by the New York City League of Women Voters in 1979. The City Charter, which had been amended in 1975, decentralized a number of important government functions and the delivery of services. The book informed New Yorkers about those changes–enabling them to affect decisions that would have an impact on their lives.

In the introduction to the 1979 edition, we said that "writing an up-to-date, accurate description of New York City government is like trying to paint a picture of a perpetual-motion machine because the city doesn't stop running long enough to make a definitive statement." That assessment proved correct and the book was revised and updated on three separate occasions.

In 1988 and again in 1989, the voters approved amendments to the New York City Charter that more radically altered the structure of city government than have any changes since 1898 when the five boroughs were chartered by the State of New York to create a unified city. The major change was the elimination of the Board of Estimate which, since its creation in 1902, functioned through law and custom as the most influential legislative and administrative body "in control of the streets of the city."

This new *What makes New York City run?* outlines the redistribution of the powers held by the Board of Estimate to new and existing city entities. It identifies the centers of power and the checks and balances incorporated in the newly amended City Charter that enable elected representatives and the residents of every borough, community and block to take part in the decision-making process.

The impetus for charter amendments came from a federal court opinion that the Board of Estimate, as structured, violated the equal protection guarantee of the Fourteenth Amendment to the United States Constitution; more specifically, its one person/one vote doctrine. The court ruled that giving the borough president of New York City's smallest borough, Staten Island, the same one vote on the Board of Estimate as the borough president of the city's largest borough, Brooklyn, resulted in unequal representation for Brooklyn residents. So our perpetual-motion machine is not solely governed by the provisions of our own constitution, the New York City Charter, or even by the New York State Constitution from which it derives its authority; it is also governed by the provisions of the United States Constitution.

New York City is considered by many to be the most exciting, important and complex city in the world. It is an international center for finance, commerce, the arts, fashion, sports, politics, publishing and the media. Its problems, sometimes more than its triumphs, are the lead stories in newspapers and on TV news programs across the country and throughout the world. For millions each year it's a great place to visit but for 7.3 million people in five boroughs...it's home. And New Yorkers want and need the same municipal services and access to their government as citizens in every village, town or city in the country.

As with every large city in the world, New York is confronted by enormous challenges. But it is unique in that it is often the first stop for new immigrants and the last stop for the disadvantaged. Too often it is the first victim of downturns in the national economy and the hardest hit by federal budget cuts for housing, health and human services.

These problems often appear insurmountable. The government apparatus seems so remote and bogged down in crisis that New Yorkers

Introduction

sometimes despair of effecting change. So many competing constituencies are clamoring for municipal services and access to jobs, housing, education, that average New Yorkers often feel their neighborhood, race, or ethnic group is being ignored or being discriminated against and that their needs are considered insignificant.

But that is the wonder of New York City—as new problems arise and new patterns emerge, New Yorkers have been ready to adjust the government's apparatus and revise their laws and governing documents to permit change and new responses. Even before the challenge to the constitutionality of the Board of Estimate was finally decided by the United States Supreme Court in 1989, a Charter Revision Commission, chaired by Richard Ravitch, was established in 1986 by Mayor Edward I. Koch to review the entire charter. Early on it was evident that government would be open—open about its functions and functionaries and open to equal participation by all of the diverse groups and constituencies that make up what Mayor David N. Dinkins calls "the gorgeous mosaic."

Guiding principles of both the Ravitch and later the Schwarz Charter Revision Commission included commitments to:
- fair and effective representation of the city's diverse racial and ethnic groups
- a system of checks and balances between and among different officials and government institutions
- increased accountability of agencies and officials
- a shift from crisis management to long-term planning
- an open and accessible government with increased public participation in policy decision-making

These principles are evident in such institutional changes as enlarging the City Council from 35 to 51 members, establishing new entities such as the Campaign Finance Board, the Voter Assistance Commission, the Independent Budget Office, the Commission on Public Information and the Procurement Policy Board, as well as several offices to ensure equal opportunity for minorities and women in employment and contracting.

The principles are also reflected in such new disclosure and planning documents as the contract budget, reports on social indicators and tax benefits, a ten-year capital strategy, and an annual citywide statement of needs prepared in accordance with "fair-share" criteria for the siting of city facilities, to name just a few.

As of this writing, almost all of the charter changes have been implemented although the election for the 51-member council will not take place until the fall of 1991 and there appears to be resistance to the creation of the Independent Budget Office.

Practical politics and ever-present fiscal constraints may impact on charter revision in ways neither foreseen nor anticipated. Readers need to be aware that what is "supposed" to happen, as described in this 1991 edition of *What makes New York City run?*, may in fact develop differently than anticipated, or perhaps not at all.

New York City has a larger population than any municipality in the United States and it is unique in that it contains five counties. The five counties, or boroughs, cover more than 300 square miles with more than 6,000 miles of streets that have to be paved, plowed, cleaned and patrolled. The city's fiscal year 1991 expense budget is $29 billion–larger than the national budget expenditures of Greece and Ireland combined. It is the only city in the country that supports municipal hospitals and pays part of the welfare costs of the one million residents who receive some form of public assistance. New York City has more children in its public schools than 12 states and the District of Columbia have in total population. New York City is unique, and it is big! But efficient operation of government is just as important to each of its 7.3 million residents as it is to each of the 6,000 residents of New Carlisle, Ohio or the 18,500 residents of New Canaan, Connecticut.

Why should every New Yorker understand city government and know how to participate in and influence its decisions? The answer is very simple. It is because the city's government influences every resident every day. The decisions made at City Hall, in the Municipal Building and in government offices throughout the five boroughs determine how much we pay in real estate taxes, how effectively our children are educated in the public schools, how much we pay for a subway or bus ride, how often our garbage is collected, how and where the homeless will be housed, how the sick will be cared for, and how well our neighborhoods, blocks and homes are protected.

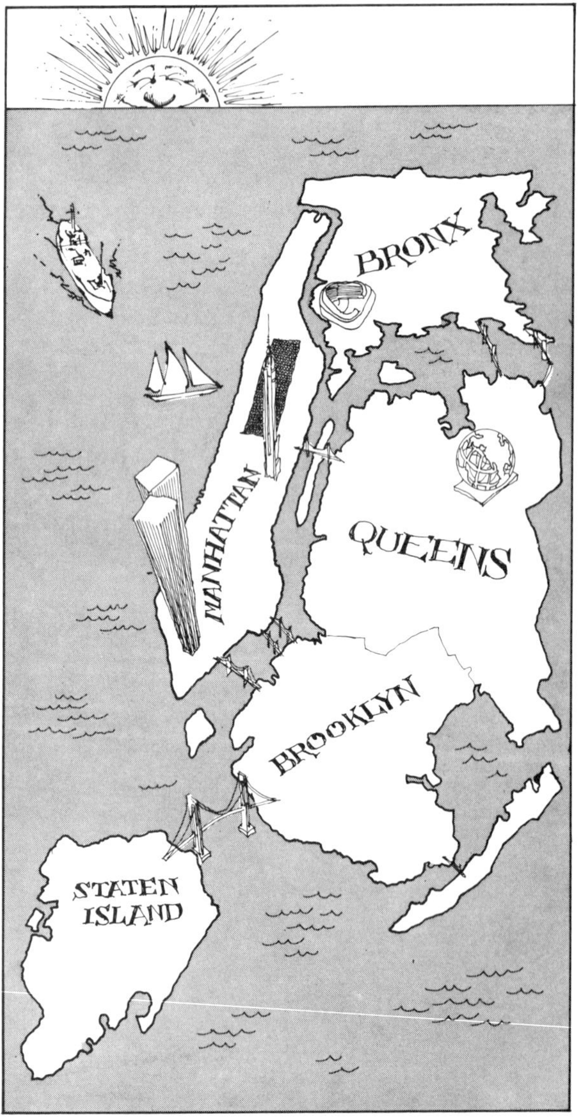
BRONX
MANHATTAN
QUEENS
BROOKLYN
STATEN ISLAND

New York City—
not an island unto itself!

Before we discuss what New York City government can do, we should understand what it can't do. New York City may be unique, but like every other city in the United States, it is not completely independent. Its legal existence depends upon the State of New York. As a local government, it gets whatever power it has from the state and that power is subject to the restrictions of the state constitution. In 1923 the Home Rule Amendment to the New York State Constitution was passed, empowering the state to delegate to cities the right to enact local laws "relating to their property, affairs and government."

Restrictions, however, still remain. New York City cannot entirely control its own finances since its power to tax and borrow is restricted. Authority to impose any taxes but real estate taxes must be granted by the state legislature and even the rate of real estate tax is limited by the state constitution.

Many programs and policies mandated by the state must be enacted and paid for by the city. For example, city schools are under the ultimate control of the state Board of Regents. The state mandates curriculum guidelines, minimum teacher-competency standards, and the minimum number of school days.

There are other areas where state law determines city action. The state Civil Service Law takes precedence over city Civil Service regulations. The Multiple Dwelling Law of the state sets minimum standards to which the city's Multiple Dwelling Code must conform. Programs in welfare and education set up by the state must be funded in part by the city and must be operated by the city. The New York City transit system is part of the state Metropolitan Transit

Authority but a portion of its cost is paid by the city.

Federal programs for welfare, housing, education, etc., while often funded at least in part by the federal government, must be administered by the city, which is accountable for disbursal of the money and maintaining standards. Many of these federal programs have stringent guidelines as to who qualifies to participate, who can be hired, and who can be helped. Many require partial city funding.

New York City government must comply with the requirements of the United States Constitution and federal laws. Even after the most recent charter amendments were approved by the voters, the amendments could not be implemented until they were certified by the U.S. Justice Department to be in compliance with the federal Voting Rights Act.

To complicate matters even more, certain city entities, such as the Board of Education and the Health and Hospitals Corporation, are quasi-independent and can make many internal decisions without the approval of city government.

Since the fiscal crisis of 1975 the city has been subject to review and audit by a state-created control board. Initially, the Emergency Financial Control Board was empowered to exercise controls and supervision over the financial affairs of the city. In 1978, the name was changed to the Financial Control Board and, while it now reviews the financial plan of the city on a post-audit basis, it can become an active player in the city's budget process if the budget is more than $100 million out of balance or if the city is facing other fiscal crises.

All of this may lead New Yorkers to conclude that the city is powerless, but this is certainly not the case. Severe as all these restrictions may be, the daily delivery of services–police, fire, sanitation, parks, etc.–is still the responsibility of the city government and these services vitally affect New Yorkers' lives. Even with all the restrictions and guidelines, the city sets the priorities. With X dollars available, the city decides how many police will be hired, how many firehouses will be maintained, how much money will be given to the Board of Education, and how often the garbage will be collected. The city, despite various limitations, possesses the power to regulate the broad range of activities that occur within its boundaries.

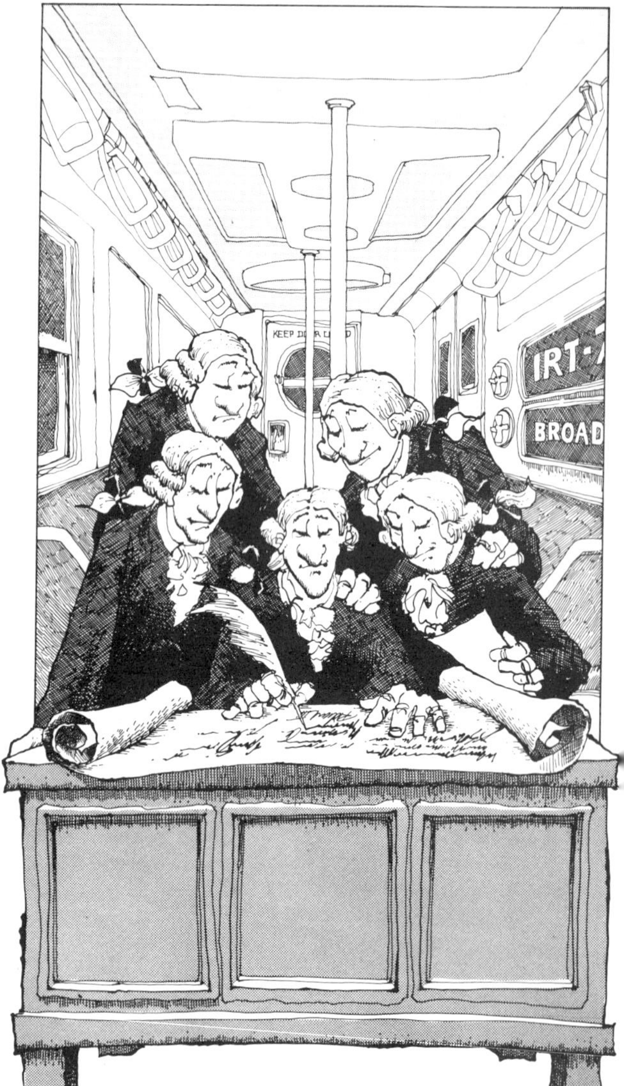
IRT-7
BROAD

What makes New York City run? the Charter!

The Charter Revision Commission, appointed in December 1986 and chaired by Richard Ravitch, was directed by statute to look at the entire charter and not limit its review to the Board of Estimate, the constitutionality of which was under judicial review. While the commission began its work and organized a series of public hearings to ascertain the views of New Yorkers, the city continued its appeal of the original federal court decision that the voting structure of the Board of Estimate was unconstitutional. In 1988, the U.S. Supreme Court agreed to hear the case, and the Ravitch Commission decided to postpone consideration of altering the Board of Estimate or redistributing its powers to the mayor, City Council or City Planning Commission until the case was decided. Instead, the commission proposed a series of charter amendments that would reform city government without changing its basic governmental institutions. These amendments were overwhelmingly approved by the voters in the 1988 election.

Charter Amendments Approved in November 1988

Voters approved a series of amendments in November 1988 that established:

- a standard of ethics and disclosure procedures to be followed by city officials and enforced by an independent five-member Conflicts of Interest Board
- a Campaign Finance Board to carry out the local law on public financing of campaigns for all elective offices, including the City Council (the law was implemented for the first time in the 1989 elections)

Provided for:
- a nonpartisan Voter Assistance Commission, composed of city officials and community and civic organization representatives, to encourage and facilitate voter registration and encourage participation in elections
- a "Tax Tribunal" to hear appeals on such nonproperty taxes as the unincorporated business tax, commercial rent tax, real property transfer tax, utility tax, and the commercial and passenger motor vehicle tax

Other amendments:
- required that all city agencies develop and annually update plans for maintaining the city's infrastructure and major capital assets (the mayor must prepare an annual report to accompany the executive budget explaining any lapses in planned infrastructure maintenance)
- set up a process for determining when a mayor is temporarily or permanently unable to perform the responsibilities of office
- replaced the practice of filling vacancies in the city's elective offices by automatic succession or appointment with nonpartisan, specially called elections
- required a uniform and clear process for the promulgation of rules by city agencies and for their publication
- reorganized and simplified the charter and removed inappropriate gender references

The Charter Commission appointed in 1986 officially went out of business after voter approval of these amendments in 1988. But it was reconstituted in January 1989 with a new chair, Frederick A.O. Schwarz, Jr., and four new members on the 15-member commission. The Schwarz Commission quickly set upon its task to examine the operation and structure of New York City government. Another series of public hearings was scheduled. Each function of city government was researched and options for change were prepared and discussed.

On March 22, 1989, the U.S. Supreme Court ruled unanimously that the Board of Estimate, as constituted, was unconstitutional. While the commission was not mandated to eliminate the Board of Estimate, any plan that emerged would have to comply with the one person/one vote principle and with the provisions of the federal Voting Rights Act requiring protection of the voting rights of minorities.

As you will note in the pages that follow, the revised charter, which evolved from the work of this commission, did much more than eliminate the Board of Estimate and redistribute its powers. It restructured New York City government, and:

- enlarged the City Council and increased its powers,
- expanded the required disclosure of information,
- increased local involvement in land-use planning,
- created mechanisms designed to reduce the possibility of corruption in government, and
- changed the contracting procedures.

As of May 1991, the changes proposed by the commission, and approved by the voters, have yet to be fully realized. Many required rules and regulations are in place but have not yet been tested. What is essential is that New Yorkers understand their own vital role in the city's "perpetual-motion machine." They need to know how, when and where their voice can be heard, which buttons to push and how loud or often to complain. We hope this League publication will do just that.

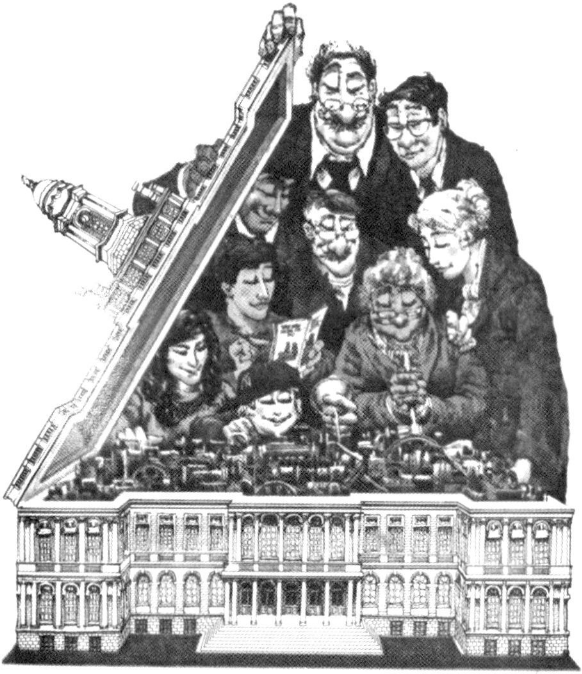

Who makes New York City run?

All New York voters elect three citywide officials (the mayor, the president of the City Council, the comptroller) as well as a borough president and a City Council member every four years. They all run at the same time, but are independent of one another. A system of checks and balances is in place to assure a degree of independence that is of special importance in a city where almost all officeholders historically are members of the same political party.

The Mayor

The charter provides for a strong mayor and explicitly says: "The mayor, subject to this charter, shall exercise all the powers vested in the city, except as otherwise provided by law." Obviously, this is a far-reaching mandate. The mayor appoints one or more deputy mayors, the heads of all city agencies, except where otherwise specified in the law, and may make most appointments without approval of the City Council (see section on the City Council for exceptions). The mayor must sign every bill for it to become a law, but the mayor's veto may be overridden by a two-thirds vote of the City Council. He or she proposes the city's budgets to the City Council, is responsible for the operation of the city and the delivery of city services, and is responsible for developing strategic policy for the city.

The mayor's appointees serve at the pleasure of the mayor, subject to dismissal at any time. In other words, the health commissioner, the fire commissioner, the sanitation commissioner and others are responsible only to the mayor—not to the City Council or directly to the voters.

The Mayor

The mayor appoints all commissioners of agencies as well as:

- 7 of the 13 members of the City Planning Commission, including the chair
- 3 of the 5 members of the Procurement Policy Board
- 2 of the 11 members of the Commission on Public Information and Communication
- 7 of the 15 members of the Districting Commission which, following each 10-year federally conducted census, divides the city into districts for the election of City Council members
- The chair and 2 of the 5 members of the Campaign Finance Board
- 3 of the 9 appointed members of the 16-member Voter Assistance Commission
- All 5 members of the Conflicts of Interest Board, with the advice and consent of the council

The mayor is given extensive power to create, merge, reorganize or abolish major mayoral agencies. These reorganization plans become effective unless disapproved by the council within 90 days of receipt.

Budgets

The mayor proposes an executive budget, which includes the expense and capital budgets as well as a contract budget for the city. The *expense budget* provides for day-to-day operating costs, while the *capital budget* provides for construction and physical improvements in the city. The City Council may increase, decrease, add or omit items in the budget. The mayor may veto any increases or additions, and that veto is subject to override by two-thirds of the City Council. However, the mayor may not veto any decrease made in the budgets by the City Council.

The *contract budget* gives the City Council and the public an understanding of how much will be paid for services contracted out by the city and how many consultants will be hired. It includes only personal service, technical and consultant contracts let by agencies. Contracts for the purchase of supplies, materials and equipment are not included. For example, the itemization of the Board of Education's contracts includes those let for pupil transportation, but not for the purchase of books.

Planning Documents

Every four years the mayor is required to submit a *strategic policy statement* delineating the long-range issues facing the city and the policy goals and plans to deal with these issues. In order to balance local and borough perspectives with those of the city as a whole, the mayor must take into consideration the strategic policy statements of the borough presidents in formulating this statement.

The mayor is also required to submit a *ten-year capital strategy*, which is updated in each odd-numbered year, describing the strategy for the future development of the city's capital facilities. This strategy includes the goals, policies and criteria for assessing capital needs, as well as a projection of the anticipated sources of revenue to finance the strategy and a description of its potential social, economic, and environmental effects. The ten-year capital strategy is developed from the preliminary strategy prepared by the Department of City Planning and the Office of Management and Budget and takes into consideration any capital plans prepared by the borough presidents.

The mayor is also responsible for preparing an annual *report on social indicators*. This report analyzes the social, economic, and environmental issues facing the city and proposes some strategies for dealing with the issues that emerge from this analysis.

The mayor must also prepare and submit to the City Council an annual *tax benefit report*, listing all tax abatements, exclusions, exemptions and credits to permit clear cost analyses of these benefits. This report should clarify the real cost to the city of the many tax abatements and exclusions now permitted. These include senior citizen real estate tax exemptions, as well as more controversial benefits such as those designed to encourage economic development and housing.

Management Reports

In addition, the mayor must make public and submit to the City Council, by January 30 of each year, a *preliminary management report* on the goals and actual performance of each agency as well as a proposed program for the following year. For example, the Department of Transportation may report on how many potholes they plan to fill and how many streets they plan to pave, how well they fulfilled the past year's goals, how much they spent to pave the streets, who received the contracts to do the paving, and whether or not the work was satisfactory.

The mayor's management reports must also include schedules of agency service goals, performance standards and actual performance relative to goals for each agency program or service provided to a local service district within a community board's area or within a borough. These reports are applicable to those city agencies that provide services through local districts and are very valuable sources of information on how community districts are faring in receiving city services. Agency reports on the community districts' expense budget items and service information are included in a *district resource statement* (DRS), prepared annually by the Office of Management and Budget. The DRS includes information on personnel, equipment, agency performance, and contractual services.

Mayoral Inability or Succession

The charter contains a prescribed plan for dealing with the temporary or permanent inability of the mayor to carry out the duties of the office, and establishes an Inability Committee to make this determination. The committee includes the comptroller, corporation counsel, a borough president, the council speaker, and a deputy mayor selected by the mayor. Four of the five members would have to declare the temporary or permanent inability of the mayor to serve. Should the mayor subsequently state his or her intention to resume the duties of the office, disapproval by four of the five members of the Inability Committee would be required to prevent the resumption of office. If the mayor challenges the decision of the committee, a two-thirds vote of the council would be needed to uphold the committee.

The president of the City Council is first in line to become mayor and the comptroller is second. The successor serves until the next general election, at which time a new mayor is elected. If neither of these officials is able to serve, a successor will be elected by a majority vote of all of the members of the City Council. If the vacancy in the office of mayor occurs before September 21 in any year, the vacancy will be filled in the general election held in that year. If the vacancy occurs after September 21, the vacancy will be filled in the general election in the following year.

The President of the City Council

The president of the City Council is another of the three citywide officials elected every four years by all voters.

The council president presides over council meetings and votes in the council in case of a tie. The charter also provides for the council president to succeed to the mayoralty until the next general election when the mayor's office becomes vacant.

The council president is charged with monitoring the operations of the public information and service complaint programs of city agencies. He or she receives, investigates and attempts to resolve individual citizen complaints, and may investigate patterns of complaints. The council president may also hold public hearings on the performance of city agencies in providing services, responding to public concerns, and complying with the City Charter.

By October 31 of each year, the council president must provide the council with a report on the year's activities of the council president's office, including a statistical summary of complaints received, and recommendations for administrative, legislative or budgetary resolutions. The report is also to include information on any charter requirements that are not being implemented by city officials or agencies, improvements in charter compliance since the last report, recommendations for improvements and the fiscal implications of those recommendations.

This citywide overview of agency performance and charter compliance can be very beneficial to the public as another vehicle for evaluating agency effectiveness. While the first avenue for reporting service complaints is with community boards (see p. 40), when these complaints are handled exclusively on a local level, widespread patterns of problems do not necessarily emerge. The council president's ability to hold public hearings, receive the testimony of commissioners and issue reports is intended to inform the public and to assist elected officials who vote on agency appropriations.

The President of the City Council

- Chairs the Commission on Public Information and Communication
- Appoints one member of the City Planning Commission
- Appoints one member of the Contract Performance Panel
- Serves on the special committee that appoints the director of the Independent Budget Office
- Makes recommendations for appointments to the Task Force on Service Delivery (see p. 43)

The Comptroller

The comptroller of the City of New York is elected every four years at the same time as the mayor and the president of the City Council. As an independently elected official, the comptroller advises the mayor and the City Council on the financial condition of the city and recommends fiscal policies and financial transactions for the city.

One major power of the comptroller is the ability "to audit and investigate all matters relating to or affecting the finances of the city." This authority extends to any public or private agency operating with city funds. The comptroller is not limited to determining if an agency is using public funds in the most efficient and economically effective way, but may also determine if the programs are achieving the "desired goals, results or benefits." The comptroller is the caretaker of the city's money–arranging for the sale of city bonds, certifying the city's expenditures and administering the city's bank accounts, sinking funds and trust funds.

The comptroller also can object to the registration of a city contract if he or she believes that corruption is involved in the letting of the contract. While the comptroller's action cannot formally cancel the contract award, the mayor is required to respond to the comptroller's objections. After responding to the comptroller's objections in writing and indicating what corrective actions will be or have been taken, if any, or why the mayor disagrees with the comptroller's objections, the mayor may require that the contract be registered despite the comptroller's objections.

The comptroller provides each city agency with a monthly summary statement of its accounts and prescribes how vouchers, payrolls and records are to be prepared. Upon finding that an agency is abusing its authority to issue vouchers or has insufficient internal financial controls, the comptroller may, with the approval of the Audit Committee, suspend or withdraw this authority.

The charter also mandates the comptroller to publish a full report of the receipts, expenditures, and cash balance or surplus of the city within four months after the close of the fiscal year.

The charter is very specific about what this statement must include: the average daily collected deposits in bank accounts, the investment performance of the city pension funds, an itemized statement of all taxes due and uncollected at the end of the fiscal year, the reserves for uncollectible taxes, the uncollected parking-violations receivable and the sources of city revenue, just to mention a few items.

By March 1 of each year, the comptroller must provide the mayor and the City Council with a report of all major audits undertaken by his or her office during the previous fiscal year. This report is useful in preparing and approving the subsequent year's budget. The comptroller also establishes a regular auditing schedule for city agencies to assure that one or more aspects of an agency's program is audited at least once every four years. This provides another opportunity for New Yorkers to learn about the effectiveness of city programs.

Independent Audit

The charter requires an annual outside audit of the city's books. The independent accounting firm hired to conduct the audit is selected by the Audit Committee. The committee also approves the comptroller's selection of an outside actuary to review the soundness of the city's pension systems.

The Audit Committee

- The mayor
- The comptroller
- Four private members with financial and accounting expertise (all are appointed by the mayor, two upon the recommendation of the comptroller)

The Borough Presidents

Each of the five boroughs has a chief executive officer–the borough president–elected at the same time as the citywide officials to serve a four-year term.

Borough presidents have been part of city government since the five boroughs were unified into one municipality in 1898, but the extent of their power has fluctuated with each revision of the City Charter. The 1963 revision of the charter resulted in decreased administrative power, while the 1975 Charter decentralized the delivery of certain city services along community district lines, giving the borough presidents added influence over the provision of services in their boroughs. By eliminating the Board of Estimate, the drafters of the 1990 Charter ended the legislative function of the borough presidents but authorized a number of other responsibilities which give residents, through their borough presidents, a role in shaping the future of the borough and improving the delivery of local services.

As mandated by the 1990 Charter, borough presidents participate in the budget-making process of the city. Each appoints one member to the City Planning Commission and to the Board of Education, appoints all members of local community boards and chairs a borough board. The borough presidents are also directly involved in land-use planning and service delivery for their respective boroughs.

The mayor is mandated to consult with the borough presidents in the preparation of the city's budgets. Five percent of the capital budget and 5 percent of the non-mandated increases in the expense budget must be allocated to the borough presidents, as a group, for their respective programs and projects. The City Council also has to consult with the borough presidents when considering the budgets. Each borough president can propose legislation for consideration by the City Council and can appeal City Planning Commission land-use decisions affecting the borough to the City Council.

Services in the Boroughs

The borough president reviews the allocation of resources and personnel of the city agencies delivering services to community districts and can request the reallocation of these resources and personnel within the borough. The borough president may also review the performance of contractors who receive city funds for projects or services in the borough and recommend modification, termination or nonrenewal of such contracts.

The borough president coordinates a borough-wide citizen complaint program and makes recommendations to the mayor and the president of the City Council on patterns of problems in the borough.

All land-use decisions affecting the borough are subject to review by the borough president and he or she can propose sites for city facilities within the borough. If the borough president opposes a site selection and has recommended an alternate site, the original application will require a super-majority vote of the City Planning Commission for approval. A super-majority comprises 9 of the 13 members.

The borough president also participates in developing the scope of environmental impact statements prepared for projects which come under the Uniform Land Use Review Procedure (see p. 64). The borough planning office assists in planning for the growth and development of the borough and provides technical assistance to community boards. The borough president can also propose changes in the city's Zoning Resolution.

Every four years, the borough president is required to prepare a strategic policy statement for the borough which is then considered by the mayor in the preparation of the city's strategy statement.

The Borough President

- Recommends to the mayor nominees for the Task Force on Service Delivery
- Sits on the Franchise and Concession Review Committee when it reviews proposals for the borough, and participates on the Off-Track-Betting Site Selection Board when it is considering OTB locations within the borough
- Collectively, the five borough presidents appoint one member of the Commission on Public Information and Communication, and one of the borough presidents serves on the special committee to select the director of the Independent Budget Office

Each borough president maintains a topographical bureau, headed by a director who serves as construction coordinator and consulting engineer, to monitor capital projects in the borough. The director can serve as an expediter and provide technical assistance on construction projects.

The City Council

Assuming the 1991 redistricting goes according to schedule, in November 1991 voters will elect 51 City Council members who will begin a two-year term in January 1992. In the November 1993 municipal election, candidates for the City Council will be on the ballot again. Those elected will serve for four years, returning the council election to the original four-year cycle.

Voters in each council district elect one council member. When a vacancy occurs during the term of office, the charter provides for a nonpartisan election to fill the vacant seat.

The council sets its own rules and procedures, establishes committees, and passes its own budget. The first meeting of the council must be held on the first Wednesday after the first Monday in January, at noon. Beyond that, the charter stipulates only that there must be at least two meetings a month, except in July and August. The mayor may also call special meetings of the council. All council meetings are open to the public, and the council is required to publish an agenda at least 36 hours prior to a scheduled meeting and as early as possible before a special meeting. The charter requires that transcripts of all council hearings be available to the public.

The council elects a speaker from among its members. The speaker is the operational head of the council—hiring the professional staff, setting meetings, directing the preparation of the rules, and assigning chairs and members to the many standing committees. Although none of these functions are mentioned in the charter, they nonetheless give the speaker extensive authority and power to determine the council's agenda. While the charter provides for council approval of committee chairs, members and procedures, in practice the process is controlled by the speaker. In order to limit the power of any one individual, the charter provides mechanisms for a sponsor to get a bill voted on in committee, and for a majority of the council members to vote to discharge a bill from committee so that it can be voted on by the entire council.

The City Council adopts all local laws and the city's budgets. It can review land-use matters and oversee all city programs and agencies. The council sets the annual real estate tax rate and can levy other taxes if approved by the state legislature. It also passes Home Rule Messages which request the state legislature to pass laws to benefit the City of New York.

The City Council member is the citizen's closest elected representative to city government, and is funded to maintain an office in the district he or she represents. The council members closely interact with the local community boards, of which they are nonvoting members. They also recommend half of the community board members to the borough president, who makes the actual appointments. The recommendations are apportioned according to the population represented by each council member in the board's district.

Each local law passed by the council can cover just one subject. Every proposed law or budget modification introduced in the council must be accompanied by a *fiscal impact statement*. This cost estimate of legislative action is designed to foster fiscal accountability.

For a legislative proposal (a bill or intro) to become law, it must be approved by a majority vote of all council members and signed by the mayor. If the intro is vetoed, it is returned to the council with the mayor's written objections, and the council has 30 days to reconsider or override the veto by a two-thirds majority. If the mayor takes no action within 30 days after receiving it from the council, the bill is considered approved.

Local laws that change basic provisions of the charter, such as the composition of the council, creating a new elective office or abolishing or transferring the power of any elected official, must be approved by the voters of the city in a referendum.

The City Council has sole jurisdiction over passage of the city's budgets—the expense budget, the capital budget and the contract budget. It is important to note at this point that throughout the year the mayor, comptroller, borough presidents, and the Independent Budget Office present financial reports and statements to the council in preparation for the council's final consideration of the budgets.

The council must approve every budget modification that varies from the original budget authorization by 5 percent or $50,000, whichever is greater. In addition, if the mayor wants to impound budgeted funds and not spend them for the purpose authorized, prior notification and explanation must be given to the council.

City Planning Commission land-use decisions relating to zoning, housing, urban renewal plans and projects, as well as those plans for the growth and development of the city and most dispositions of city-owned residential property, automatically go to the City Council for approval, disapproval or modification. Other City Planning Commission decisions, including special zoning permits, sites for capital construction projects such as jails and shelters, and the disposition of city-owned, nonresidential property, are subject to council review if the affected borough president or community board objects to the plan or if a majority of the council votes to consider it. The council has 50 days to approve or disapprove a decision of the planning commission and 65 days if it proposes a modification.

The council, or any standing committee of the council, has the power to "investigate any matters within its jurisdiction relating to the property, affairs or government of the city...." In addition to its investigatory and oversight authority over city agencies, their programs and their spending patterns, the council is directed by the charter to review the city's procurement policies and procedures. The charter specifies that this review include the rules and procedures adopted by the Procurement Policy Board, the rules relating to the participation of minority- and women-owned businesses in the city's procurement process, and the procurement practices and spending patterns of city agencies.

While the mayor appoints the heads of most agencies without approval from the council, mayoral appointment of the following officials requires the advice and consent of the council: the commissioner of investigation, members of the Art Commission, Board of Health (other than the chair), Board of Standards and Appeals, City Planning Commission (other than the chair), Tax Commission, Taxi and Limousine Commission, and the public members of the Environmental Control Board. The council must hold a public hearing within 30 days of receiving the nominations. If it does not act within that time period, the appointment is deemed to be approved.

The council appoints the city clerk, who serves a six-year term, and is the custodian of the city's papers and documents.

The Districting Commission

Over the years, citizens and good government groups have criticized the political redistricting of the council as a process that protects incumbents and the majority political party.

The charter now mandates creation of a 15-member Districting Commission with specific directives for its composition and authority.

Appointments to the 15-member Districting Commission

- 5 members, one from each borough, appointed by the delegation of the council's majority political party
- 3 members, each from a different borough, appointed by the council's minority political party
- 7 members appointed by the mayor

  The commission elects a chair from among its members.

The commission must include representatives of the city's racial and language minorities, as defined by the Voting Rights Act, in proportion to their numbers in the population. No single political party can have a majority of the votes.

The charter is also very specific about the districting criteria. Each district:

1. may differ by no more than 10 percent of the average population for all districts;
2. must ensure fair representation of racial and language minority groups protected by the U.S. Voting Rights Act of 1965, as amended;
3. must be contiguous and, if separated by water, connected by bridge, tunnel, tramway or ferry;
4. should keep intact neighborhoods and communities with established ties of common interest;
5. should not cross borough boundaries, unless unavoidable, in which case no more than one district can include territory from the same two boroughs, and
6. should not be drawn to separate geographic concentrations of voters enrolled in the same political party.

Finally, while the council can disapprove the proposed districts and the commission must reconsider its plan based on the council's objections, the commission–not the council–has the final authority to adopt the districting plan, subject only to clearance by the U.S. Justice Department.

The Community Boards

In describing who makes New York City run, we have so far focused on elected officials. The appointed, nonsalaried volunteers who serve on community boards also play a major role in the process. Community boards have been in existence since the early 1960s, and in Manhattan since 1951. Since January 1977 there have been 59 community boards, each comprising up to 50 members appointed by the borough president of the borough in which the board is located. One-half of the appointees to each board are nominated by the City Council members whose districts coincide with the board's district. The number of nominees allotted to each council member is proportionate to the population represented by the council member. Appointed community board members serve staggered two-year terms, one-half of the members appointed each year. The council members whose districts coincide with the board's area are ex-officio community board members without a vote.

A chair is elected by the board from among the members. The community board has a budget to hire a district manager and staff.

Community boards represent constituencies as large as some American cities, up to 250,000 residents. The districts are supposed to be compact, contiguous, and suitable for the efficient and effective delivery of services. The charter mandates a review of the district lines in 1993 and every 10 years thereafter.

The boards' responsibilities and prestige have increased with each revision of the charter. They have become important forums through which community residents can make their needs and concerns known.

The community boards set budget priorities for their districts and provide the mayor with an annual statement on recommendations for programs, projects or activities to meet their district's needs. They monitor the delivery of city services in their districts and are the first governmental body to vote on land-use proposals which go through the Uniform Land Use Review Procedure (ULURP). Community boards have the authority to submit their own plans for growth, development and improvements in their communities.

While they have always been able to make recommendations for land use in their communities, the boards have had to use their own resources to prepare an environmental impact statement. Now, if the City Planning Commission determines that the plan meets certain standards, an environmental impact analysis of the plan will be prepared through the Office of Environmental Coordination.

The land-use review process ensures public awareness of, and community participation in, planning and development decisions. Concerned community residents no longer have to find out about a new building on the block the day the foundation goes in. For example, if a developer wants to build a high-rise apartment complex in an area zoned for low-density buildings, the community board will hold a public hearing on the application and the residents can testify.

The boards are required to keep public records of their activities and transactions, including minutes of their meetings.

Citizens may attend and testify at all public hearings and may be appointed as members of community boards or, on some boards, be appointed as public members to the standing committees that serve the boards. For information on how to be appointed to your community board, write to your borough president or City Council member.

Coterminality

Community and borough boards not only provide local communities with the tools to set local budget priorities, make land-use recommendations and find local solutions to their problems, but also to monitor and improve service delivery. These services are provided by agencies through districts that share borders with the community board district. To assist them, the charter mandates a district service cabinet in each community board as well as a borough service cabinet for the corresponding borough board.

The District Service Cabinet

- Chair of the community board
- District manager, who serves as chair of the service cabinet
- Representatives of government agencies delivering such local services as:
  Police
  Sanitation
  Social Services (Human Resources Administration)
  Parks and Recreation
  Youth Services

The district service cabinet coordinates the delivery of services in the district area. This process is facilitated by having the agencies listed above share service delivery boundaries with community board lines. In addition, many other services are coordinated around the boundaries of several community boards, such as Housing Code enforcement, street and sewer maintenance and some health and housing facilities, other than municipal hospitals.

These coterminous (shared boundaries) service lines serve two purposes for the community. They make it easier for the service providers to cooperate with the community's representatives and with each other, and they make it possible for the residents of a community to go to one place with their city service problems.

The borough service cabinet, chaired by the borough president, coordinates service delivery functions and agency programs at the borough level. The charter requires the head of each city agency that provides these services to appoint borough commissioners, with authority over agency programs, personnel and facilities, to consult regularly with the borough presidents and sit on the borough service cabinets.

To assure compliance, the charter requires the mayor to appoint a 10-member Task Force on Service Delivery to review the services provided along district lines. The task force can recommend changes in the list of coterminous services or in the requirements for such services. Task force members are appointed upon the recommendation of the council, comptroller, president of the council and borough presidents. The mayor is required to report to the council every two years on the quality and implementation of service delivery in the boroughs and districts.

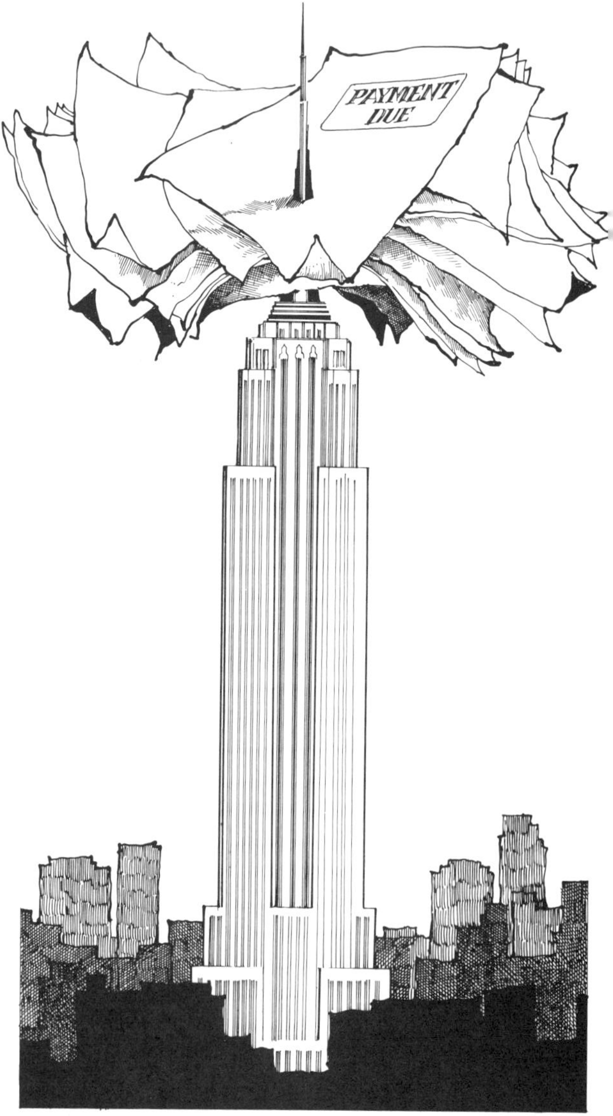
PAYMENT
DUE

How New York City plans its spending—the budgets

A budget is more than an accounting tool—it is a public statement reflecting the priorities and political philosophies of the mayor who proposes it and the council which passes it. While most items in the budget are mandated, such as cost-of-living increases and labor contract provisions, the unmandated appropriations are subject to policy considerations. When there is a budget surplus, should taxes be lowered or services increased? When there is a fiscal crisis, should the budget be cut to decrease all services proportionately, or are some programs more vital than others? While the average New Yorker may not understand or feel competent to question the accounting principles of the budget, every New Yorker has a preference for which services are most needed or most desirable, and it is through public participation in the budget-making process that these needs and desires can be most effectively expressed.

New York City functions through two budgets, a day-to-day operating or expense budget, and a borrowing or capital budget.

It is through the *expense budget* that the city pays for employee salaries, supplies, rent, utilities, programs and the interest incurred from short-term loans and bonds issued by the city to pay for capital improvements. The money used to pay for items in the expense budget comes from city taxes, fees and other local revenues and from state and federal aid.

It is through the *capital budget* that the city borrows money for construction and physical improvements such as street and park repairs, reconstruction of tunnels and sewers, and the purchase of equipment and machinery.

The charter also requires the mayor to submit a separate *contract budget* with the expense budget, which goes into detail on the programs, services or studies that will be performed by contractors. Contractual services are those that are performed by consultants, nonprofit agencies or businesses outside of city government. While the contract budget describes the services that will be contracted, the contracts are subsequently drawn up and the vendors selected by the city agencies under the direction of the mayor's Office of Contracts, in compliance with the guidelines established by the Procurement Policy Board.

Although the city's fiscal year begins on July 1 and ends on June 30, the budget-making process is a year-round exercise. Each successive charter has provided new mechanisms to encourage public participation in the process and to facilitate informed legislative consideration of budget proposals.

Throughout the year, the comptroller, borough presidents, city agency heads, including the director of the Office of Management and Budget and the commissioner of finance, local community boards and the Independent Budget Office report to the mayor and to the City Council on the financial condition of the city and the implementation and management of budgeted programs. From these reports and estimates, the mayor fashions a *preliminary budget*, including the expense, capital and contract budgets. Each unit of appropriation in these budgets must be accompanied by a statement of its programmatic and financial impact. The mayor presents the preliminary budget to the City Council by January 16 of each year. At the same time, the mayor must submit to the council a *preliminary report of the capital debt and obligations* and estimate how much the city may expend for capital projects and still stay within its debt limit.

The council and community boards review and hold hearings on the preliminary budget. The mayor may modify the budget after receiving more recent financial reports, revenue estimates and actual appropriations from the state and federal governments, and may make changes based on persuasive arguments for special needs from agency heads, community boards, interest groups and the public.

By April 26 of each year, the mayor submits to the council the *executive budget*, which is based on revisions of the preliminary budget. The executive budget must be accompanied by a *budget message*, which explains the major programs, projects and objectives, together with information on the financial and economic condition and tax and fiscal base of the city. The mayor must also provide, among other items, a four-year financial plan, an itemized statement of the city's entire capital plant, and explanations of any modifications made to the preliminary budget. The expense budget includes the City Council's operating budget which must be included as passed by the City Council.

As indicated in the section on the borough presidents, 5 percent of the non-mandated increases in the mayor's expense budget and 5 percent of the capital budget are allocated to the borough presidents, collectively, for borough programs and projects. Each borough president can also propose modifications to the preliminary budget to reallocate appropriations within the borough. However, when the borough president recommends an increase in one appropriation, it must be offset by a decrease in another. In other words, the borough presidents can propose shifts in borough programs but not increases in total budget appropriations. In the budget message, which accompanies the mayor's executive budget, the mayor must explain any changes in the borough appropriations previously proposed and the borough president's modifications to the preliminary budget. The borough presidents can then respond to the mayor's executive budget and ask the City Council to address their proposed modifications in the council's final budget considerations.

Beginning in 1991, the Independent Budget Office* must publish a report, by May 15 of each year, analyzing the executive budget for the ensuing fiscal year. Between May 6 and May 25, the City Council holds public hearings on the executive budget to which it can summon agency heads, community leaders and community and borough board representatives to testify.

The council may modify the mayor's budget but each increase or decrease must be for a single item or purpose and, in total, the budget cannot exceed anticipated revenues. The appropriations for capital projects must not exceed the maximum amount of debt and reserves that the mayor has certified the city can soundly incur for capital projects.

By June 5 of each year, the council adopts the budget which becomes effective July 1. The budget does not have to be signed by the mayor, as do city laws.

Unlike the federal and state prohibitions on continued spending if budgets are not passed, the city can continue spending money without a continuing resolution even if the fiscal year ends without a budget being passed. If the budget is not passed by June 5, the expense budget and tax rate of the current budget are in effect for the fiscal year beginning July 1 until the new budget is passed. The unutilized portion of the current year's capital budget is to be reapportioned until a budget is passed for the new fiscal year.

While the mayor's approval is not required to implement the budget, the mayor may veto any additions or increases that the council approved but which were not in the mayor's executive budget. The mayor has five days from the date of passage of the budget to disapprove the changes by providing a written explanation to the City Council. The council may override the

---

*office not established as of May 1991

mayor's veto by a two-thirds vote of all of the members. If the council does not take action on the disapproval (veto) within 10 days, the budget as modified by the mayor is deemed adopted.

The following schedule for budget and financial submissions, as specified in the charter, illustrates how the budget is formulated, and indicates when the public can participate in the budget-making process.

Budget Calendar

While the charter specifies budget calendar dates, these dates are subject to change. Complex budget negotiations, changes in economic conditions, unanticipated revenue shortfall or delays in passage of the state budget, which affect anticipated city revenues, can all affect the city budget calendar.

by January 16

The mayor submits the preliminary budget to the City Council. The mayor submits a preliminary report of the capital debt and obligations and of the city's reserves, and estimates how much the city can expend for capital projects and stay within its debt limits for the following fiscal year and each of the three fiscal years after that. The preliminary report is submitted to the council, comptroller, borough presidents and City Planning Commission.

by February 1

The Independent Budget Office reports on the estimated expenditures and revenues for the coming fiscal year. Each community board holds a public hearing on the preliminary budget statements with respect to the needs and priorities of the district.

no later than February 15

Each community board submits a statement of its budget priorities and recommendations to the mayor, City Council, borough president, director of the Office of Management and Budget and each member of the borough board.

The commissioner of finance reports to the mayor and the council on an estimate of the assessed valuation of taxable property and the amount of all property taxes due. The mayor submits a tax benefit report to the council, listing all exclusions, abatements, credits and other tax benefits.

by February 25

Following one or more public hearings, each borough board submits a comprehensive statement on the budget priorities of the borough to the mayor, council, and director of the Office of Management and Budget.

by March 1

The comptroller presents to the mayor and the council a certified schedule for paying interest on the city's debt.

by March 10

The council submits its operating budget to the mayor. The borough presidents submit their modifications of the preliminary budget to the mayor and the council.

by March 15

The Independent Budget Office issues a report analyzing the preliminary budget.

by March 25

The City Council, as a whole or through its committees, holds public hearings on the preliminary budget requests, the statements of budget priorities of the community boards and borough boards. The public can testify at these hearings.

by April 26

The mayor submits the executive budget to the council.

by May 6

The borough presidents submit their comments on the executive budget to the mayor and the council.

How New York City plans its spending 51

by May 15
The Independent Budget Office publishes a report analyzing the executive budget (see p. 55).

May 6 to May 25
The City Council holds public hearings on the executive budget.

by June 5
The council adopts the budget.

by June 10
The mayor must submit to the City Council a written explanation of any disapproved increases or additions to the budget adopted by the council.

by June 20
The mayor's disapproval may be overridden by a two-thirds vote of all of the members of the council. If the council fails to act by this date, the budget, as modified by the mayor's disapprovals, becomes the adopted budget.

by July 1
The new fiscal year begins and the budgets are in effect.

Even after the budgets are adopted, they are still subject to change as the year progresses. The charter says that any modification of any unit of appropriation of 5 percent or $50,000, whichever is greater, must be submitted by the mayor to the City Council. The council has 30 days to disapprove the proposed modification unless it is in a borough allocation and has the approval of the borough president. If the borough president proposes modification of an appropriation and the mayor concurs, City Council action is not needed.

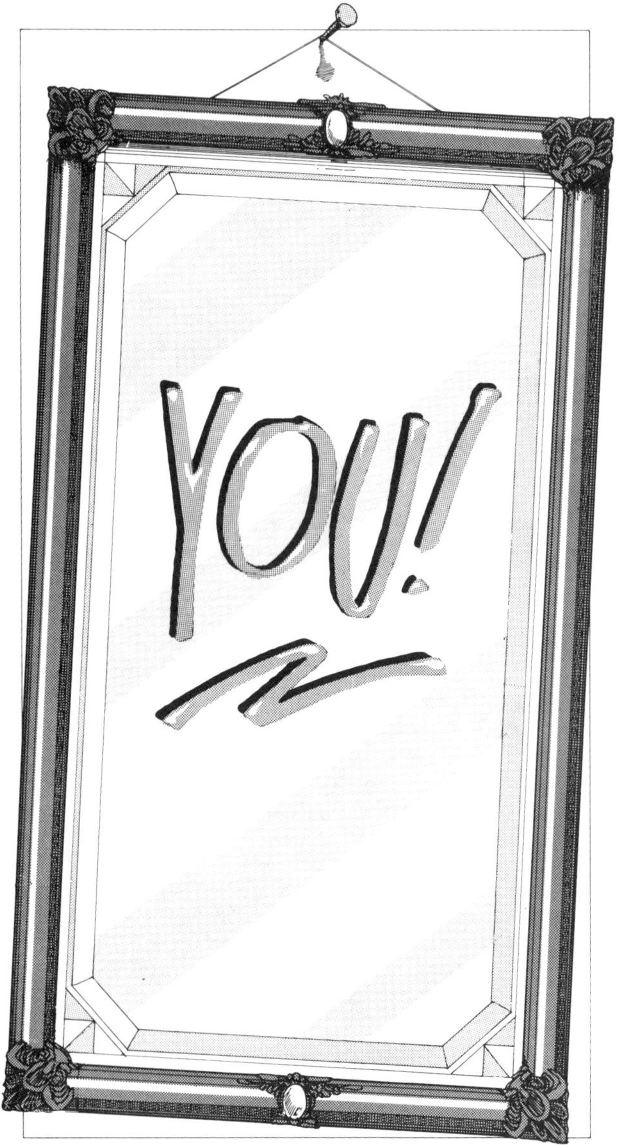
YOU!

Who pays for New York City government?

The Sources of Revenue

The simplest answer to "Who pays for New York City government?" is you! Every New Yorker pays for city services through taxes: sales tax, income tax, real estate tax, and a variety of business and commercial taxes. Some of the taxes New Yorkers pay to the state and federal governments come back to the city in the form of aid.

More than 65 percent of the funds used to pay the city's expenses come from revenues raised by the city alone. About 25 percent of that amount comes from property taxes, and 40 percent from other taxes and miscellaneous revenues. The remainder of the funds come from the state and federal governments, some in the form of unrestricted grants, and most through categorical state and federal aid. Categorical aid is aid given for specific purposes and must be used within a given formula for such purposes as Medicaid or public assistance.

Since the state legislature authorizes the city to increase taxes and also passes on aid to localities upon which New York City depends, the city budget process is heavily dependent upon the resolution of the state budget. The state's fiscal year begins April 1, which means that preparation of the city's preliminary budget precedes passage of the state budget. When the city's budget passage is delayed, the current year's expenditure and tax rate remain in effect. But when the state's budget is delayed beyond the start of the state's fiscal year, the state has no budget–aid to localities stops or is delayed. For the city this may mean added borrowing, and interest payments, to make up for the temporary loss of state aid.

Crisis Management

From the onset of the city's fiscal crisis in 1975, the city was unable to raise money for capital projects or pay off debts through the sale of city bonds and notes, the traditional form in which cities raise money. To enable the city to meet its capital needs, the state created the Municipal Assistance Corporation (MAC), which for 10 years sold bonds for the city, backed by the state's credit.

Since 1985, the city has been back in the traditional financing market but the Municipal Assistance Corporation remains in existence to direct the repayment of the bonds it sold. The MAC debt was refinanced at a lower rate and a surplus resulted in the MAC fund. However, the corporation has put conditions on the release of these funds to the city, limiting the way in which the money may be spent.

In 1975, the state also created the Emergency Financial Control Board to monitor the city's expenditures and financial plans. "Emergency" was removed from its title when that fiscal crisis passed and the board adopted an advisory role and limited its review of the city's finances to an audit of the city's spending and revenue. However, the board's role can change if the city has a deficit of $100 million at the end of a fiscal year, if it can't pay the principal or interest on its debt, if the city and state comptrollers say that the city can no longer borrow money, or if the city does not follow mandated accounting practices.

The Financial Control Board has seven members: the governor, the mayor, the state and city comptrollers, and three private citizens appointed by the governor, with the advice and consent of the state senate.

The Independent Budget Office*

After years of being subject to financial scrutiny by state and federal entities, New York City will have its own charter-mandated fiscal watchdog—an Independent Budget Office (IBO). This office will serve as a nonpartisan, truly independent, well-funded participant in the budget process.

The Independent Budget Office will provide the council, comptroller, borough presidents and community boards with information on the preliminary and executive budgets, the fiscal implications of local laws and proposed legislation, estimates of revenues and changes in financial conditions. The IBO is guaranteed a budget of at least 10 percent of the appropriations available to run the city's Office of Management and Budget.

The director of the Independent Budget Office is selected by majority vote of a special committee composed of the comptroller, council president, a borough president chosen by the other borough presidents and a council member chosen by the council. The director is appointed without regard to political affiliation and serves for a four-year term that overlaps the terms of the appointing officials. Additionally, a 10-member Independent Budget Office Advisory Committee is appointed by the comptroller and president of the council for staggered five-year terms. The charter requires that its members have extensive experience in finance, economics, accounting, public administration and public policy. The committee selects its own chair from among the members, who are non-salaried and cannot serve consecutive terms.

All of these provisions are designed to ensure the independence and expertise of the IBO and to remove this office from partisan considerations and "power plays" often associated with the budget process.

*office not established as of May 1991

The Financial Information Services Agency

Throughout these sections on sources of revenue and spending, we have indicated how the charter provides for the issuing of reports, estimates, standards, and the publication of financial information–all intended to open the fiscal process to public scrutiny.

The Financial Information Services Agency is another link in this chain. It consists of three directors appointed by the mayor, one of whom has been recommended by the comptroller. FISA is charged with implementing and managing "an integrated financial management system" in city government–or more to the point, with ensuring that the city follows sound and generally acceptable accounting practices.

How contracts are awarded

Each year, New York City awards more than $6 billion in contracts for goods, service and construction projects performed by outside contractors. This amount of money is greater than the entire budgets of some countries and many states. But the process for awarding these contracts has been fragmented, confusing and frustrating for city agencies and contractors, and virtually incomprehensible to the general public. The City Charter now requires consistent procurement policies and procedures to be followed by all city agencies.

The Procurement Policy Board
- 3 members appointed by the mayor
- 2 members appointed by the comptroller

The mayor designates the chair.

The Procurement Policy Board establishes the guidelines for agencies to follow in soliciting bids, determining the responsibility of the bidders and resolving contract disputes. The mayor's **Office of Contracts** oversees the contracting and procurement activity of city agencies, maintains a comprehensive contract management information system (Vendex), and trains agency procurement personnel.

While the Procurement Policy Board establishes policy and guidelines for awarding contracts, subject to approval by the City Council, the agencies award the contracts and the mayor is accountable for them.

The charter specifies the different ways to award contracts: competitive bids, sealed bids, small purchases, sole source contracts and other alternative procurement proceedings. The

Procurement Policy Board formulates and publicizes the rules for these procedures.

- All contracts exceeding $10,000 must be publicly advertised.
- Noncompetitively bid contracts for more than $100,000 require a public hearing by the agency awarding the contract, except in an emergency.
- The mayor, or a deputy mayor, has to sign off on all contracts of more than $2 million.
- The comptroller must register every contract and can object within 30 days of the awarding of a contract.
- The comptroller also audits all contracts on a regular basis.

As part of the borough president's oversight responsibilities regarding service delivery, 120 days before the expiration of a contract, the borough president may recommend modification, rejection or termination of a contract in the borough. The agency has 10 days to respond to the borough president's recommendation. If there is no response or if the response is unsatisfactory, the borough president may, within 30 days, convene a Contract Performance Panel in the borough consisting of the mayor, comptroller and president of the City Council, or their designees. The panel hears testimony and makes a finding on the disposition of the contract.

The charter also mandates creation of a certified computer data base of all city contracts and contractors, including performance evaluations. It requires public access to copies of all contracts.

The Procurement Policy Board is charged with establishing a prompt payment schedule. The prompt payment program may require the city to pay interest to contractors who are not paid in a timely fashion. While prompt payment is a concern of all parties and has discouraged some from doing business with the city, small businesses and locally based social service providers are particularly disadvantaged by late payments.

Another charter-established resource for small-business people is The **Office of Economic and Financial Opportunity** (OEFO), which is charged with facilitating the participation of minority- and women-owned businesses and locally based small businesses in the city's contract process. The OEFO provides information, education and technical assistance for these owners to participate in the city's procurement programs.

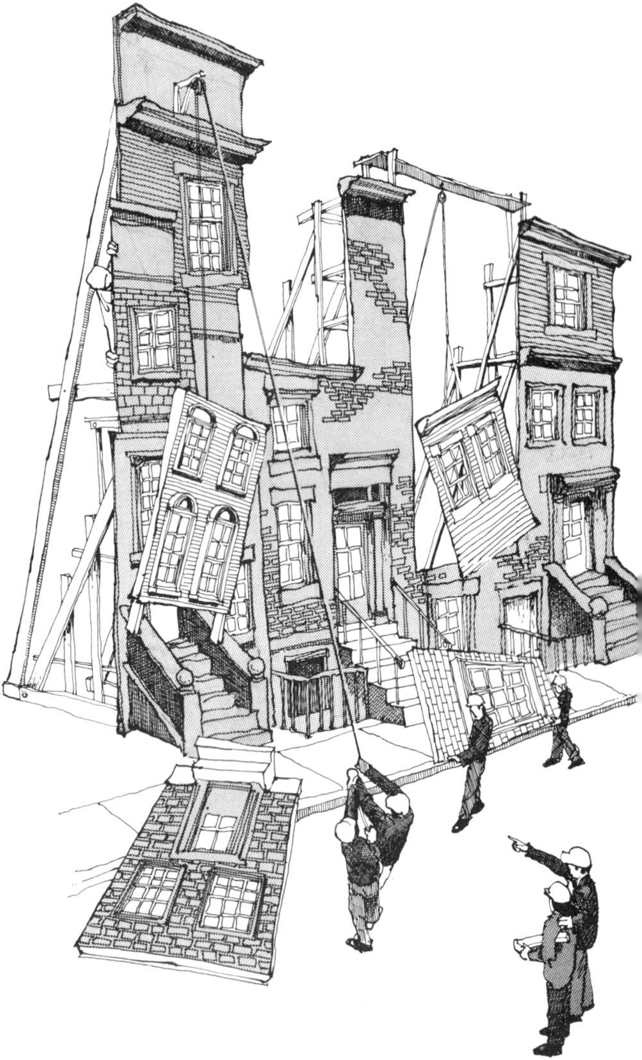

Land Use and City Planning

The use and development of city land is one of the most important and contentious issues facing the city. New York City doesn't have any wide-open spaces or new frontiers to develop, so deciding how to use land is really a process of substituting one use for another. Each use has its advocates and its detractors. How land is used determines the city's tax base and the availability of housing, recreational facilities, business, jobs and social services. It determines the economic and social condition of the city.

Each charter revision introduced new mechanisms to provide opportunities for communities to participate in the local land-use decision-making process while maintaining a structure to allow for the orderly, necessary growth and development of the city. The search for the optimum balance of local interests with that of the borough or city as a whole remains a difficult one.

The City Council makes the final decision on land-use and development projects but, prior to council consideration, there are extensive rules and specific schedules in the charter for action by community boards, borough boards, borough presidents, the mayor, the Department of Environmental Protection, the Department of City Planning, the City Planning Commission, the Landmarks Preservation Commission and the Franchise and Concession Review Committee.

The **City Planning Commission** and the **Department of City Planning**, headed by the chair of the City Planning Commission, are the city's professional planners and the pivotal players in the complicated land-use process.

The City Planning Commission
(13 members)

- 7 appointed by the mayor, including the chair
- 1 appointed by the president of the City Council, with the advice and consent of the council
- 5 appointed by the borough presidents—one from each borough

  All appointments, except the chair, are subject to confirmation by the City Council. The members serve five-year staggered terms and cannot hold any other city office.

Each borough president appoints a member to the City Planning Commission but, once designated, the member is supposed to be independent and not serve solely as the borough president's representative on the commission.

According to the charter, the City Planning Commission is "responsible for the conduct of planning relating to the orderly growth, improvement and future development of the city, including adequate resources for the housing, business, industry, transportation, distribution, recreation, culture, comfort, convenience, health and welfare of its population." To appreciate the scope of this charter-mandated planning process, remember that we're talking about a city which encompasses over 300 square miles inhabited by more than 7.3 million people, with buildings, bridges, parks and streets, many of which are more than 100 years old, and with whole communities whose development dates back to the eighteenth and nineteenth centuries.

The City Planning Commission assists the mayor in developing the ten-year capital strategy, the four-year capital plan and the annual statement of needs. Every two years the commission must file a zoning and planning report with the mayor, council, president of the council, borough presidents and community boards.

The chair of the commission, who is also the head of the Department of City Planning, and the commissioner of the Department of Environmental Protection assign staff to an **Office of Environmental Coordination**. This office assists city agencies as well as community boards, borough boards and borough presidents in fulfilling their environmental review responsibilities. The City Planning Commission also establishes rules and minimum standards for plans for development, growth and improvement of the city, boroughs or community districts. Community boards, borough boards and the borough presidents can also propose such plans. Any such plan is subject to public hearings by the affected community board(s) and the borough board prior to hearings before the City Planning Commission and/or the City Council.

The Department of City Planning is the operational, administrative arm of the commission. Every application subject to review under the Uniform Land Use Review Procedure (ULURP) must be made to the Department of City Planning before it is reviewed by the affected community board, borough board, borough president and relevant city agencies.

Uniform Land Use Review Procedure

The applications and plans subject to ULURP are those that:

- change the city map,
- require the sale, lease or acquisition of city property, other than for office rental,
- change or subdivide streets, or public places,
- require zoning changes or special permits,
- involve site selection for capital projects,
- involve revocable consents and franchises,
- concern housing and urban renewal plans,
- involve landfills.

Other matters involving the use, development or improvement of property, as proposed by the City Planning Commission and enacted by the City Council, may also be subject to the Uniform Land Use Review Procedure.

The Department of City Planning certifies that land-use applications, or plans affecting the items cited above, are complete and ready to proceed through ULURP. In response to concern that this precertification process could be endless and unreasonably delay projects, the charter permits an applicant or a borough president to petition the City Planning Commission to act on the certification if the process has not been completed within six months of filing of the application.

Once certified, the application starts the ULURP clock, which involves preparation of an *environmental impact statement*, hearings and recommendations by affected community and borough boards, hearings and votes by the City Planning Commission, and final approval or disapproval by the City Council. There is a specific timetable in the charter for this review process but it may be modified and delayed if additional information is required. The charter mandates that the affected community board may participate in planning the scope of the environmental impact statement.

Council Review

The City Council automatically reviews City Planning Commission approvals that affect:

- city zoning changes,
- the disposition of city-owned residential property,
- plans for housing and urban renewal, and
- plans submitted by the mayor, borough presidents or community boards.

While these ULURP decisions are automatically subject to council review, other land-use decisions can be appealed to the council for consideration if a majority of the council members vote to consider the issue at the request of the affected borough president and community board. The decisions which can be reviewed under these circumstances are:

- decisions on site selection for the city's capital projects,
- disposition of city-owned property (except office leases),
- city map changes, and
- waterfront and sanitary landfill subdivisions.

Every public hearing in the review process provides an opportunity for local residents and affected parties to observe, testify or submit written testimony. The charter requires public hearings by community boards, the City Planning Commission and the City Council. This means that, at the minimum, New Yorkers have three opportunities to participate in the process.

PUBLIC REVIEW UNDER UNIFORM LAND USE REVIEW PROCEDURE

Community Board Receives Certified Application from Dept. of City Planning. Community Board Has 60 Days to Hold Public Hearing and Make Recommendations to Borough President and City Planning Commission

↓

Borough President (and Borough Board if More than One District Affected) has 30 Days to Hold Public Hearing and Make Recommendations to City Planning Commission

↓

City Planning Commission Has 60 Days to Hold Public Hearing. Can Approve, Modify or Disapprove by Majority Vote

↓

City Council Can Review City Planning Commission Approvals If:
- the application concerns zoning changes, urban renewal plans, disposition of City-owned residential property;
- a Borough President Requests such Review, and both the Borough President and Community Board Recommended Against Approval ("triple no");
- the Council votes by majority within 20 days to Review the Application ("call up")

↓

City Council Can Review City Planning Commission Denial of Zoning Amendments and Special Permits, If Mayor Files Certificate of Necessity with the Council

↓

Mayor Can Veto City Council's Decision, or, If Council has Failed to act, the Mayor Can Veto Planning Commission's Decision

↓

Council Can Override Either Veto with a 2/3 Vote

Reprinted by courtesy of the Municipal Art Society of New York

Fair Share Siting

The mayor is required to develop criteria for the siting of public facilities and for expanding, reducing or closing existing facilities. Many facilities vital to the city are considered undesirable by their neighbors. Very few people want to live next door to a landfill or a sewage treatment plant. Shelters and prisons are not readily welcomed by communities. On the other hand, few communities want to lose a firehouse or a hospital. Local residents often are resentful of what they see as a concentration of "undesirable" facilities in their neighborhood or the unannounced closing of a "desirable" facility. The criteria for siting city facilities developed by the City Planning Commission are to ensure a "fair distribution among communities of the burdens and benefits associated with city facilities, consistent with community needs for services." The impact of these facilities on the surrounding area must also be taken into account. This process should improve community understanding and increase community participation in decisions affecting public facilities.

By November 15 of each year, the mayor is required to prepare a *citywide statement of needs* which explains the rationale and implications for the siting, expansion, reduction or closing of city facilities proposed for that year. The statement is submitted to the council, borough presidents, borough boards and community boards for review, comment and recommendations. The borough president can also propose locations for any new city facilities to be sited in the borough or recommend an alternative site to the one proposed by the mayor, as long as the site meets all established criteria. When a city agency acts on the statement of needs, the borough president's recommendation must be taken into consideration.

The citywide statement of needs is accompanied by an Atlas which maps and lists all city-owned or leased property within each community board. There is an Atlas for each borough.

The Board of Standards and Appeals

The Board of Standards and Appeals is another player in the land-use process. The six-member board makes, amends, repeals and enforces regulations relating to the construction of all buildings in the city, and hears and decides appeals and requests for variances on these matters. The board sets the standards for all buildings and appliances used in New York City construction. It also grants variances and some special permits under the Zoning Resolution regulating private properties.

The board circulates the applications and supporting documents for variances and special permits to affected community boards and borough boards for review, public notice and, if desired, public hearing. The community's comments and recommendations are forwarded by the Board of Standards and Appeals to the City Planning Commission. However, the board makes the final decision. Its decisions are not subject to review by any other legislative or executive body, but may be appealed to a court of competent jurisdiction.

The Landmarks Preservation Commission

The Landmarks Preservation Commission designates buildings and sites as landmarks. Once designated, these buildings cannot then be renovated or changed without the approval of the commission. The commission's procedures, therefore, are designed to protect landmarks without infringing too drastically on the rights of ownership.

Over the years, there has been an increasing trend to designate entire blocks or neighborhoods as historic landmarks. While acknowledging the desirability of preserving historic buildings, some have challenged this process as a way to restrict or discourage development rather than to preserve that which is truly historic. The 1990 Charter more directly involves the City Planning Commission in the process of designating historic districts and requires the commission to hold a public hearing on each such designation. The City Council, by majority vote, has the authority to modify or disapprove a landmark designated by the Landmarks Preservation Commission. If the designation is vetoed by the mayor, the council may override the veto within 10 days.

On occasion, the commission determines that a building should be landmarked, despite owner opposition. Sometimes religious or other tax-exempt institutions argue that their finances or declining membership prevent them from maintaining the property in its current state and want to be able to renovate, demolish, or sell the air rights to build over the structure. Such activity would be severely restricted or precluded with landmark status. Tax-exempt organizations are the only entities that may appeal landmark designation to a hardship panel of five members appointed by the mayor.

Franchises, Revocable Consents and Concessions

We have addressed development, siting of city facilities, zoning changes and landmarks. The final pieces in this land-use puzzle are franchises, revocable consents and concessions.

A *franchise* is a grant by an agency to use city property to provide a public service. Cable television, which runs its cables through the city streets, is franchised, as are privately owned bus companies that provide service on city streets. Franchises that have land-use implications must go through ULURP.

The mayor and the responsible city agency have a role to play before a franchise is awarded, but only the City Council can authorize the awarding of a franchise. The mayor and the agency initiate the "authorizing resolution" which defines the type of franchise and any terms and conditions to be met. The council, after a review and public hearing, may modify or disapprove the resolution which in turn could be vetoed by the mayor, subject to override by a two-thirds vote of the council. If the authorizing resolution is approved, the responsible agency selects the specific franchisee by preparing appropriate solicitations and requests for proposals (RFPs). The proposed franchise agreement is then subject to the review and approval of the Franchise and Concession Review Committee.

A *revocable consent* is a grant made by the city with any person or persons to use pipes, conduits and tunnels under railroad tracks or on bridges or over city property. These consents are granted to private utilities, such as Con Edison, Brooklyn Union Gas and telephone companies, and can be revoked at any time. Revocable consents are awarded after public hearing by the Department of Transportation, with the exception of consents for telecommunication purposes granted by the Department of Telecommunications.

A *concession* is a grant made by a city agency for the private use of city-owned property for which the city receives compensation. Examples of concessions range from newsstands, flower stalls, hot dog stands and sidewalk cafes to the food concessions in city parks or in Shea and Yankee Stadiums.

The Franchise and Concession Review Committee adopts rules and procedures for granting concessions through public bidding or an alternative, fair competitive process. It also reviews and approves the selection of franchisees and the granting of concessions.

The Franchise and Concession Review Committee

- The mayor, who serves as chair
- The director of the Office of Management and Budget
- The corporation counsel
- The comptroller, and
- One other member appointed by the mayor

Whenever the committee reviews a franchise or concession, the borough president of the affected borough serves as a member of the committee. The affirmative vote of five members is necessary to approve a franchise agreement.

Open and Participatory Government

Earlier, we explained the concern of the Charter Revision Commission that New York City have an open government with records and transcripts accessible, understandable, and available to the public. Council, City Planning Commission, community board and borough board meetings are open to the public.

The charter has several additional provisions to ensure compliance with this mandate. A **Commission on Public Information and Communication** was established to educate the public about the availability of documents, and to assist agencies in facilitating public access to their transcripts and records. The commission is developing a plan to cablecast sessions of the City Council and City Planning Commission.

The commission is directed to publish an annual directory of the computerized information produced or maintained by city agencies.

The charter also establishes an **Office of Telecommunications**. This office is charged with planning and coordinating the telecommunications policy for the city and developing municipal uses of cable television. The office administers the franchises and revocable consents relating to telecommunications. Also, all future cable television franchises and franchise renewals must include provisions for channels to be designated for governmental use.

In recognition of the significant number of non-English-speaking New Yorkers, an **Office of Language Services** in the mayor's Office of Operations, originally established by executive order, is now mandated by the charter. It helps city agencies provide services in languages other than English and translate written materials into other languages.

The most basic way in which a citizen can participate in government is through voting.

Traditionally, voter assistance has been provided by the Board of Elections, by political parties, and by nonpartisan citizen-education organizations such as the League of Women Voters.

While that is still true, the charter established a 16-member **Voter Assistance Commission** to promote voter registration and voting in New York City. The commission comprises city officials and public representatives of groups who are underrepresented among registered voters. The commission is charged with monitoring the city's voter assistance efforts, receiving citizen complaints, and designing and conducting activities to encourage and facilitate voter registration and voting in New York City.

The charter also established a five-member **Campaign Finance Board** to administer the city's campaign finance laws. The board distributes public funds to candidates for city offices who have agreed to limit campaign contributions and expenditures in return for receiving public financing to supplement the funds they raise privately. The board is also charged with improving public awareness of candidates, proposals and referenda in all city elections through the publication of a nonpartisan, impartial voter's guide. Prior to each city election, a voter's guide is mailed to every household with registered voters.

Conflicts of Interest

In order to promote public confidence in government, the charter includes stringent provisions on what constitutes conflicts of interest by public officials and employees and on how financial disclosures must be made.

The **Conflicts of Interest Board** provides clear guidance regarding prohibited conduct of public servants. The board collects and monitors financial disclosure forms filed by city officials and issues advisory opinions on individual questions regarding conflicts of interest. The board also receives public complaints, holds hearings, and may direct the Department of Investigation to pursue any complaint or potential conflict by a public servant.

The charter prohibits public officeholders from simultaneously holding political party office. It prohibits former public employees from appearing before their former boards or agencies for one year after they leave public service. For some high-ranking public officials, that ban is extended to any city agency or board and permanently prohibits their involvement with a city agency or board on matters in which they were involved while working for the city. These prohibitions are intended to deter the "revolving door" practice that permits, in fact or perception, former public officials and employees to profit from their tenure of public service.

Among the prohibited activities for public employees are: taking any action that benefits a firm in which the public servant has an interest; engaging in any activity that is in conflict with the proper discharge of his or her official duties; disclosing any confidential information relating to the property, affairs or government of the city that is not available to the public unless the public servant has cause to believe that such information involves waste, inefficiency, corruption, criminal activity or conflict of interest; receiving valuable gifts or accepting compensation for representing private interests before a city agency; and, coercing any other public servant to participate in political activities.

There are additional prohibitions and exceptions to these rules where certain interests are disclosed and where financial interest is minimal. The charter also provides for penalties, forfeiture of pay and suspension or removal from office for prohibited activities, and establishes the rules, exceptions and procedures for disclosure.

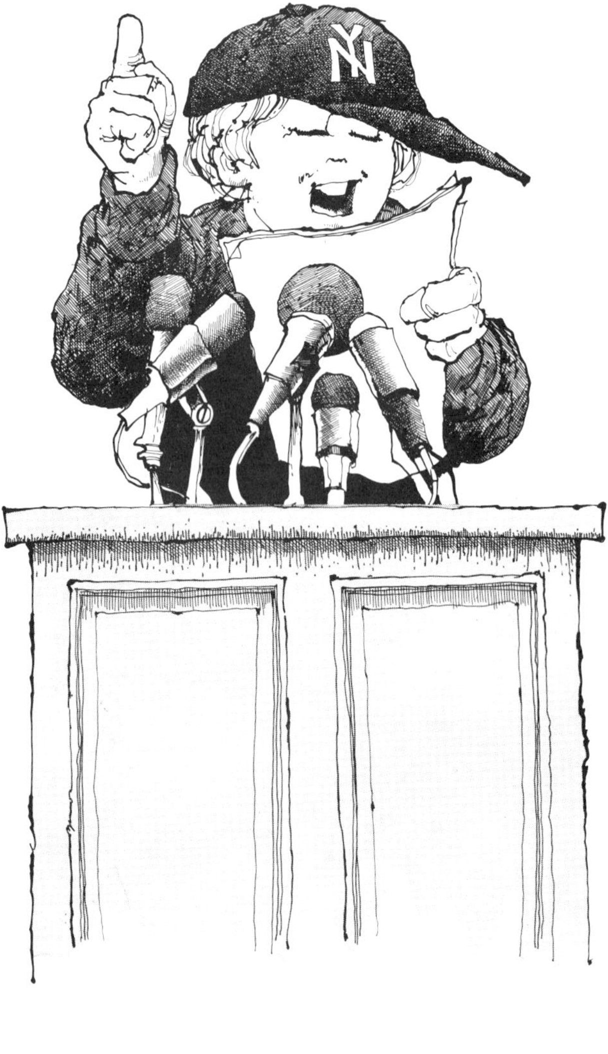

Public Hearings

Throughout this book we have referred to public hearings as a mechanism for citizens to express their concerns and needs to their representatives. However, some skeptical New Yorkers question how much effect these hearings actually have. The fact is that many decisions have been made or reversed as a result of public hearings...firehouses have been kept open, school-crossing guards have been rehired, and housing complexes have been built or canceled. On the other hand, controversial actions may have been taken–because of a lack of public expression.

If testifying is new to you, you might prepare by attending a public hearing of a City Council committee or community board, and by following some simple procedures:

- Call the public agency which is holding the hearing to find out the ground rules: How much time will you have to speak? Will you be given an approximate time slot on the agenda, or is it first come, first served?
- Always arrive a little earlier than scheduled in case the agenda has been moved up or earlier witnesses have not appeared.
- Be prepared to stay. Hearings often run behind schedule.
- Be ready with multiple copies of your written testimony for panel members and the media.
- Stay within the allotted time, which is usually from three to five minutes. Your written testimony may be as long as you like.
- State your most important arguments first, in case you run out of time. Be concise. Try not to repeat what others before you have said.
- Be prepared to answer questions.
- Sometimes an official is called away from a hearing and is replaced by a staff member. Don't be discouraged. Staff members are usually very knowledgeable and will inform officials of important testimony.

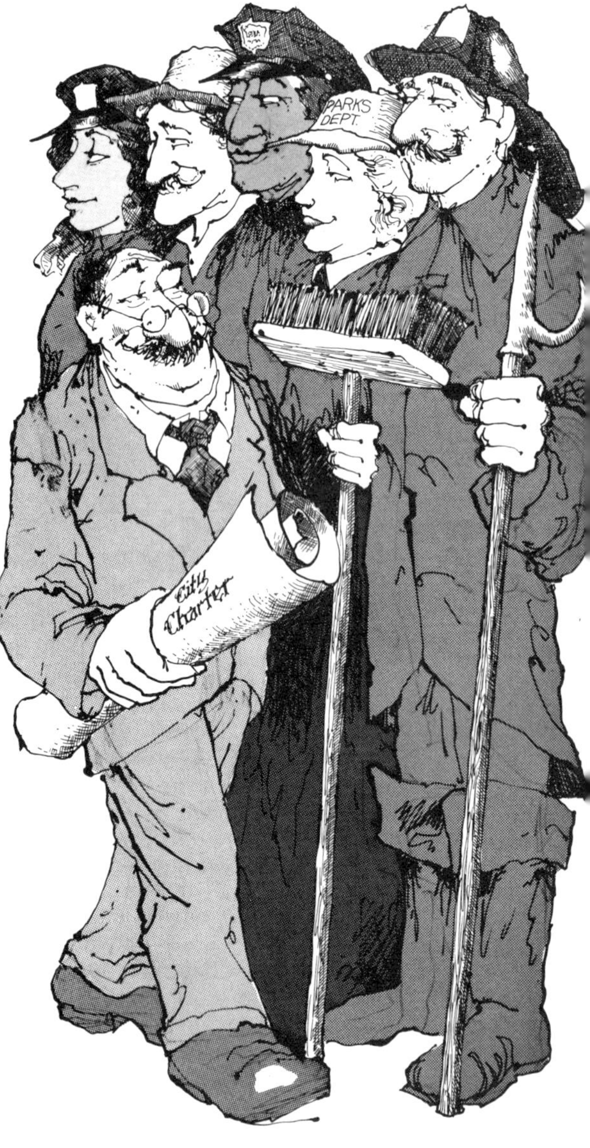
PARKS DEPT.
City Charter

City Agencies

Services are delivered in New York City through a network of city agencies. Most of these agencies are directly under the control of the mayor, who appoints the commissioners to run them. Not surprisingly, they are referred to as "mayoral agencies."

There are several "non-mayoral" agencies involved in service delivery in New York City. An agency is referred to as non-mayoral when the agency is not under the direct control of the mayor or has legislative authorization to act independently. These non-mayoral agencies include the Transit Authority, the Board of Education, the Board of Trustees of the City University and the Health and Hospitals Corporation.

In May 1991 the mayor proposed the consolidation of six development agencies, the Office of Business Development, the Office of Economic Development, the Office of Labor Services, the Department of Ports and Trade, the Public Development Corporation and the Financial Services Corporation, into two agencies—the Department of Business Services and the New York City Economic Development Corporation.

The Department of Business Services will serve as the centralized agency for all business services including technical assistance, administration of grants, neighborhood development and increasing opportunities for minority and women-owned businesses. The New York City Economic Development Corporation will serve as the city's public authority charged with development and financing of commercial and industrial development projects.

On the following pages are descriptions of some of the agencies not discussed in the preceding chapters. Most of these agencies have a direct impact on citizen needs and concerns.

The offices of the five county district attorneys, the courts, and the Board of Elections are agencies with which New Yorkers have a great deal of contact, but we will not discuss them here because they are established and administered under state law and information about them can be obtained elsewhere.

Libraries and library services are administered differently in different boroughs, and information on their services should be obtained directly from your local branch library.

Some of your problems or inquiries about city agencies can be handled through your community board office, particularly problems with agencies that provide services on community board district lines. If you have to contact any city agency directly, all of their phone numbers are listed under New York City in the blue pages of your local telephone directory.

New York City publishes and sells an official directory, known as the Green Book, which lists all city agencies, officeholders, key personnel and phone numbers.

City Agencies

We will discuss the following agencies in the order listed:

Administrative
Consumer Affairs, Dept. of
General Services, Dept. of
Management and Budget, Office of
Operations, Office of
Personnel, Dept. of
Records and Information Services, Dept. of
Voluntary Action Center

Criminal Justice
Correction, Dept. of
Juvenile Justice, Dept. of
Probation, Dept. of

Cultural Affairs
Art Commission
Cultural Affairs, Dept. of

Education
Education, Board of
City University of New York

Environment
Environmental Protection, Dept. of
Water Register, Bureau of
Environmental Control Board

Equal Opportunity
Disabilities, Office for People with
Equal Employment Practices Commission
Human Rights Commission
Women, Commission on the Status of

Finance
Finance, Dept. of
Tax Commission
Tax Appeals Tribunal

Health
Health and Hospitals Corporation, N.Y.C.
Health, Dept. of
Medical Examiner, Office of Chief
Mental Health, Mental Retardation, and Alcoholism Services, Dept. of

Housing and Buildings
Buildings, Dept. of
Homelessness and Single Room Occupancy Services, Office of
Housing Authority, N.Y.C.
Housing Preservation and Development, Dept. of
Rent Guidelines Board

Legal
Investigation, Dept. of
Law, Dept. of

Parks
Parks and Recreation, Dept. of

Social Services
Aging, Dept. for the
Human Resources Administration, Dept. of Social Services
Youth Services, Dept. of

Transportation
Taxi and Limousine Commission, N.Y.C.
Transit Authority, N.Y.C.
Transportation, Dept. of

Uniformed Services
Fire Department
Police Department
Sanitation, Dept. of

Administrative

The **Department of Consumer Affairs** enforces the Consumer Protection Law and city and state weights and measures statutes. The department licenses over 80 types of businesses. The department also conducts consumer education and protection programs and responds to citizen complaints.

A 12-member Consumer Advisory Council is established by the charter to advise the commissioner on policy, programs and studies.

The **Department of General Services** is the city's housekeeping and purchasing agency. Its **Division of Public Structures** maintains city-owned buildings, directs the construction of public structures and maintains the city's street and park lighting systems. Through the **Division of Municipal Supplies**, it purchases and stores supplies for city agencies, negotiates leases for city agencies, and is charged with the maintenance and sale of city-owned commercial property which the city acquires through tax foreclosure proceedings.

This department also runs the Municipal Broadcasting System, the City Record, and the Office of Telecommunications Control.

The **Office of Management and Budget** advises the mayor on fiscal and budget issues and develops the mayor's preliminary and executive budgets.

The **Office of Operations**, in the executive office of the mayor, coordinates and monitors agency delivery of city services. The office maintains the management report and plan system for the mayor.

The **Department of Personnel** is the city's hiring office. It classifies jobs, develops and administers competitive examinations in accordance with civil service laws, and establishes minimum qualifications for city jobs. The department investigates city-job applicants, monitors appointments and promotions, and develops training programs for city employees.

In addition, the department identifies and monitors underrepresentation of minorities and women at all levels of city government and assists agencies in developing plans to improve such representation.

The **Department of Records and Information Services** is the Municipal Archives and Records Center, and includes the Municipal Reference Library.

The **Voluntary Action Center**, an agency in the mayor's office, recruits and refers volunteers to public and nonprofit agencies in the city. New Yorkers who want to volunteer their services are encouraged to contact the center which will match their talents and time schedules with requests from public or nonprofit agencies.

Criminal Justice

The **Department of Correction** runs the city's prisons and other correctional facilities which housed approximately 21,000 inmates in 1990. The department has custody of inmates in detention awaiting trial or sentencing, those sentenced to one year or less, state prisoners with court appearances in New York City, and parole violators until their penalties are determined. Connected with the department is a separately appointed nine-member **Board of Correction** which monitors prison conditions, sets minimum standards of treatment, and hears appeals by prison inmates and guards.

The **Department of Juvenile Justice** administers the facilities for children alleged or determined to be juvenile delinquents and for children convicted as juvenile offenders. It also contracts with public and private agencies to provide services and coordinates after-care services.

The **Department of Probation** conducts pre-sentence investigations, supervises persons who are placed on probation by the courts and, in cooperation with the Board of Education, runs counseling centers for juvenile delinquents.

Cultural Affairs

The **Art Commission** reviews and approves all works of art that go in or on city buildings or property; approves the designs for buildings constructed on city property and preserves paintings and other public works of art in public buildings.

The **Department of Cultural Affairs** administers 31 city cultural institutions and works with private cultural institutions and city, state and federal agencies to promote and develop cultural activities in New York City. The department also develops, administers, and monitors cultural programs for city neighborhoods. An Advisory Commission in the agency, whose members serve without compensation, makes recommendations on the cultural activities of the city.

Education

The **Board of Education** is a quasi-independent agency. Public education is a state responsibility and the composition and mandates for the Board of Education are established by the state legislature. The board is, in general, in charge of the city's public elementary, junior high school and high school system, with some sharing of power as indicated below. The board consists of seven members, two appointed by the mayor and one by each borough president.

In most municipalities in New York State, education funds are segregated from general funds. Through a state aid formula, the legislature allocates aid to each school district. New York City is considered one school district for per-pupil allocation purposes by the state. While sizable, the state's per-pupil allocation is much less than the cost of educating a child. The state's allocation goes into the city's general fund. The city then includes educational needs as part of its expense budget and supplements the state allocation with city funds.

The city also gets some federal education funds, earmarked for such programs as educational services for disadvantaged students and the disabled, and vocational education.

The Board of Education is responsible for determining education policy for the one million children in the New York City public school system. The board employs a chancellor to administer the system. The board presents a budget to the mayor, which the mayor may increase or decrease when submitting it to the City Council as part of the executive budget. The council may also decrease or increase the total amount of the Board of Education budget, but the board has more flexibility than other city agencies in its allocation of funds. It is only in the allocation which goes to the decentralized community school districts that the council can earmark funds.

The state Board of Regents is the final authority on educational standards and curriculum requirements.

In 1969, the state legislature created community school districts (now 32) in New York City. Each community school district has a nine-member elected **Community School Board** which administers the elementary, intermediate and junior high schools in the district. The school board members, who serve for three years without salary, are residents or parents of children in the schools. All of the residents of the community school district, including noncitizen parents of children attending the schools under the jurisdiction of the community school board, may vote in the election. The elections are conducted by the proportional representation method of election, which is designed to produce more diverse and representative boards.

These boards hire community superintendents and principals, set budget priorities and make budget recommendations to the central board. They have some curriculum and program discretion but the final education authorities in the city are the chancellor and the central Board of Education. The chancellor has the power to su-persede, suspend or remove community school board members or entire boards for cause.

These community school boards offer the public local access to education policy-making. Since the community school board members are more familiar with the needs of their districts than is the central board, they can attempt to tailor programs to meet local needs within limitations set by the central Board of Education.

Community school boards hold public hearings and their monthly meetings are open to the public.

The 17-member **Board of Trustees of the City University of New York** administers the city university's graduate school, nine senior colleges, seven community colleges, a law school, a medical school and a technical school. The board of trustees submits the senior colleges' budgets to the governor, who recommends the level of state appropriation and includes it in the state budget submitted to the legislature. The board of trustees votes on tuition after the state budget is passed. The city supports the community colleges, which also receive state aid in accordance with formulas.

Environment

The **Department of Environmental Protection** (DEP) protects the city's water supply. It operates 3 upstate watersheds, 2 water tunnels, the Croton Aqueduct, more than 6,000 miles of water mains and sewers, and 14 sewage-treatment plants. It enforces the regulations for air, noise and water quality and oversees the disposal of hazardous waste and the removal of asbestos. This is the agency to contact about pollution problems and to register complaints about industrial noise, water and air pollution.

The department's **Bureau of Water Register** administers the city's water-metering program. The bureau contracts for the installation of water meters in all buildings in the city and its inspectors monitor the installation and read the meters. The rates for water and sewer usage fees are set by the city's **Water Board**. The **Municipal Water Finance Authority** floats bonds to finance improvement and construction of the system.

The **Environmental Control Board**, which is part of the DEP, regulates emissions into the air and the water within and around New York City. It enforces city rules and regulations relating to, among other things, the cleanliness of the streets; the disposal of wastes; the provision of a pure, adequate water supply; the prevention of air and noise pollution; the regulation of street peddling; the handling of hazardous wastes, and compliance with the Department of Sanitation's recycling regulations.

Equal Opportunity

The **Office for People with Disabilities** coordinates city programs for the disabled, and advocates for legislation and research to assist disabled New Yorkers. It also provides employment consultations and referral services.

The **Equal Employment Practices Commission** reviews and monitors the employment practices of city agencies and the Department of Personnel to assure equal employment opportunities for women and minorities in city agencies.

The **Human Rights Commission** is charged with preventing discrimination in housing, employment, and places of accommodation. The commission adjudicates complaints of discrimination in employment, housing, and public accommodations on the basis of race, age, gender, sexual orientation, religion, national origin, marital status, disability, lawful occupation, number of children, or conviction records, for private sector employment. Citizens can bring discrimination complaints before the commission and the commission can also study patterns of discrimination.

The commission has 15 members appointed by the mayor, one of whom the mayor designates as chair. Only the chair is a full-time, salaried employee. The commission has a salaried staff to implement its policies and programs. The commission administers Neighborhood Stabilization Project offices around the city.

The **Commission on the Status of Women** makes recommendations to the mayor for legislative or executive action to eliminate discrimination and ensure equal opportunity for women. The commission publishes material and provides programs to improve the status of women in New York City.

Finance

The **Department of Finance** enforces the city's tax laws and collects city taxes. The department keeps the tax-assessment rolls and makes annual adjustments. It also collects other city taxes and revenues, handles deposits into the city treasury and makes payments from it upon authorization of the comptroller and the commissioner of finance. The finance commissioner also monitors banks on their response to community needs and is a financial advisor for the city's pension systems.

The **Tax Commission** is charged with reviewing and correcting all assessments of real property for taxation purposes. The mayor appoints a president and six commissioners, with the advice and consent of the City Council.

Taxpayers can look at these records when they're open to the public, and if they feel the assessed valuation of their property is incorrect, they can apply for a correction.

An independent **Tax Appeals Tribunal** has jurisdiction to hear and determine appeals of nonproperty tax determinations by the commissioner of finance and can impose, modify or waive such taxes. The tribunal has three commissioners appointed by the mayor.

Health

The **New York City Health and Hospitals Corporation** was established in 1970 as a public-benefit corporation to create flexibility in running the municipal hospital system. New York City is the only major city in the country that has a municipal hospital system.

New York City has 16 municipal hospitals and runs a number of community health centers. Most of the city hospitals have an affiliation agreement with a voluntary hospital to provide back-up medical service. Voluntary hospitals are private, nonprofit institutions.

Fees for services are charged to those who can afford to pay but the only criterion for receiving treatment in a municipal hospital is medical need.

The funds to run hospital corporation facilities come from the city budget, fees for services, and reimbursement from government programs such as Medicare and Medicaid.

The corporation has 16 directors who make policy for the hospitals. Ten directors are appointed by the mayor, five of whom are designated by the City Council. The health services administrator, the commissioner of mental health, mental retardation and alcoholism; the administrator of the Human Resources Administration; the commissioner of health and a deputy mayor serve as ex-officio members. These 15 directors select a chief executive officer of the corporation who serves at the pleasure of the corporation.

The Health and Hospitals Corporation also administers the **Emergency Medical Services** which maintains ambulances and coordinates ambulance response to 911 emergency calls.

The **Department of Health** provides a range of services to assure the availability of pre- and post-natal care, child-health care, family planning, prevention and treatment of communicable diseases, medical rehabilitation, treatment of narcotics addiction, pest control, and treatment for diseases and conditions affecting public health. The department runs Child Health Centers and Children's Dental and Eye Clinics and sponsors school-based clinics. The department enforces the Health Code, inspects restaurants, and monitors blood banks and laboratories. The **Bureau of AIDS Prevention** provides counseling and testing. The Department of Health also runs immunization programs and prison health services, and maintains vital records including birth and death certificates.

The commissioner of the Department of Health chairs the **Board of Health** which oversees the implementation of the Health Code and can modify, amend or repeal sections of the Code.

The **Office of the Chief Medical Examiner** comes under the jurisdiction of the department, but the medical examiner is an independent officer. The medical examiner examines unexplained or suspicious deaths for cause.

The **Department of Mental Health, Mental Retardation and Alcoholism Services** plans, monitors, evaluates, and contracts out services for developmentally disabled and emotionally disabled children and adults. It contracts for the delivery of services with voluntary agencies, municipal hospitals and correctional facilities, and works with the courts and the Human Resources Administration.

Housing and Buildings

The **Department of Buildings** is responsible for enforcing the city's building code, zoning regulations, multiple dwelling law and labor law. This includes approval of building construction and alteration plans and inspection of buildings. The Buildings Department issues certificates of occupancy. The department has a central office and an office in each borough, and responds to complaints about structural defects in buildings. The department periodically inspects elevators and boilers in residential and commercial buildings.

An **Office of Homelessness and Single Room Occupancy (SRO) Services** in the mayor's office establishes policies and guidelines for services for the homeless and SRO tenants. It administers interagency inspections of the hotels in which homeless families and SRO tenants reside.

The **New York City Housing Authority** operates over 300 housing projects encompassing 179,000 apartments occupied by 500,000 people. The Housing Authority's police force provides security in the projects.

The authority also operates senior and community centers and administers the federally funded Section 8, Leased Housing program which assists eligible tenants with rent subsidies for housing in privately owned buildings. As of June 1990, tenants in over 45,000 apartments received Section 8 assistance.

The **Department of Housing Preservation and Development** (HPD) is charged with maintaining and improving the city's housing stock. It enforces the Housing Maintenance Code and administers emergency repair programs and relocation services. It also administers the Senior Citizen Rent Increase Exemption program. The department works to preserve and improve neighborhoods by facilitating private participation in voluntary repair programs and through the rehabilitation and development of vacant housing and new construction. It is also involved with the management and sale of city-owned residential property which the city acquires through tax foreclosure proceedings.

HPD also renovates city-owned properties for permanent and transitional housing for the homeless.

HPD's Office of Housing Maintenance, Division of Code Enforcement runs a **Central Complaint Bureau** which New Yorkers can call seven days a week, 24 hours a day with complaints about privately owned housing accommodations that have no heat or hot water, leaks, crumbling walls or ceilings, or other related housing problems.

The **Rent Guidelines Board** establishes annual levels of rent adjustments (guidelines) for rent-stabilized apartments and hotel rooms. The board has nine members appointed by the mayor. While the board establishes the annual guidelines' adjustments, the administration of rent stabilization and rent control is under the jurisdiction of the Office of Rent Administration of the Division of Housing and Community Renewal, which is a state agency.

Legal

The **Department of Investigation** may investigate the efficiency of any city agency, its personnel or any person doing business with the city. The commissioner of investigation supervises the activities of the inspectors general of other city agencies. This department also receives citizen complaints of misconduct by city employees or agencies.

The **Department of Law** is headed by the **Corporation Counsel** who, aided by his or her assistants, is the lawyer for the city and its agencies. The charter empowers corporation counsel to act in any court in the nation to "defend and establish the rights, interests, revenues, property, privileges, franchises or demands of the city" or "to collect any money, debts, fines or penalties or to enforce the laws." The Law Department also prepares and revises fiscal documents and contracts. It reviews legislation and renders legal opinions for the mayor and city agencies.

Parks

The **Department of Parks and Recreation** is responsible for the operation and maintenance of more than twenty-six thousand acres of city parks. As of 1990, this included 40 swimming pools, 511 tennis courts, 890 playing fields, 13 golf courses, 6 ice-skating rinks, 14 miles of beaches, 4 stadiums and 3 zoos. The department supervises or coordinates 22 recreational facilities, including summer play camps and programs for the disabled. It is also responsible for 700,000 street trees and 2 million park trees.

Social Services

The **Department for the Aging** plans, coordinates, and implements programs for older New Yorkers and acts as an advocate on their behalf. The department supports a series of programs directly, or through contract, to help older people remain in their communities. These services include senior centers, nutrition programs, meals-on-wheels, home care, transportation, employment and legal services. The department also provides information and referral on all rights and entitlements for the elderly.

The charter provides for a 31-member Advisory Council, at least 16 of whom shall be recipients of the services for the elderly.

The **Department of Social Services/ Human Resources Administration** coordinates the delivery of social services and provides income support to people in need throughout the city. Income support and assistance is provided to those whose low incomes make them eligible for such entitlements as public assistance, Medicaid, food stamps, rent subsidies and temporary housing in shelters.

The agency also provides (or contracts with other public and private agencies to provide) foster care, home-care services for the elderly and disabled, day-care centers, Head Start centers, services for people with AIDS, protective and preventive services for children and adults, battered women's services, employment services, and child-support enforcement assistance.

The **Department of Youth Services** develops and coordinates city agency and community youth services. Youth service programs are coordinated on community board district lines.

Transportation

The **New York City Taxi and Limousine Commission** sets the rates, service standards, driver and equipment safety regulations, and air pollution control standards for taxis, car services and limousines. It establishes the criteria for licensing the vehicles and the drivers. The commission accepts and investigates citizen complaints about driver misconduct.

The **New York City Transit Authority** is in charge of running the subways and buses. These facilities are owned by the city and leased to the New York City Transit Authority, which is an arm of the Metropolitan Transportation Authority of the State of New York (MTA). The same members serve on both authorities. The MTA was created in 1968 to coordinate public transportation in the metropolitan area.

The city's buses and subways carry, on average, 4.6 million riders a day.

About 50 percent of the operating expenses come from the fareboxes, with the remaining funds needed to run the system coming from city, state and federal subsidies.

The **Department of Transportation** maintains the city's streets, highways and bridges. It operates ferries and heliports, develops traffic-flow systems, operates municipal parking facilities and is responsible for enforcement of traffic and parking violations through the **Parking Violations Bureau**. It also regulates and monitors private bus systems.

Uniformed Services

In addition to fighting fires, the **Fire Department** is charged with enforcing fire laws and inspecting buildings for fire hazards. The department enforces the rules and regulations concerning the manufacture, storage and transportation of chemicals, explosives or flammable substances. It also investigates the causes of fires and arson cases.

The **Police Department** is charged with protecting public safety. It responds to emergency calls, investigates crimes, and maintains order at public events and demonstrations. Police-patrol service areas are coterminous with community board lines and there is a police precinct in each community board district.

Citizen complaints of police misconduct or the use of excessive force by the police should be brought to the **Civilian Complaint Review Board** of the Police Department. A complaint can be made at any police station or the board's office. The board's office is located in Manhattan, but not at police headquarters.

In addition to cleaning and sanding streets, removing snow and collecting garbage, the **Department of Sanitation** plans for, constructs and operates city incinerators and landfills and administers the city's solid-waste recycling program. It also enforces the rules governing the disposal of hazardous wastes and illegal dumping.

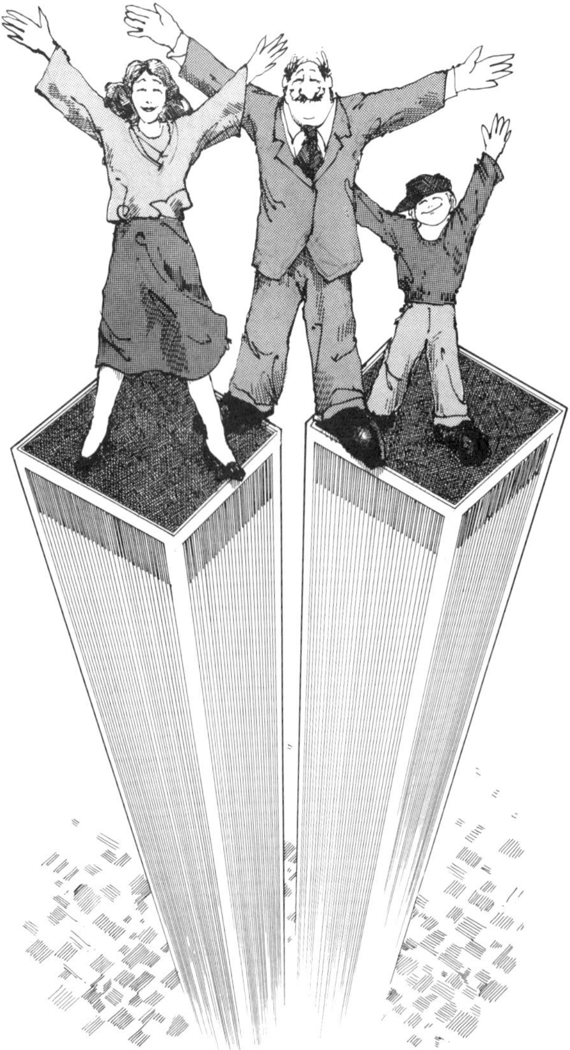

Conclusion

We hope that after reading *What makes New York City run?* you have a better understanding of our city, the services it delivers to you, the agencies that provide them and the role that you have to play in making your city work for you.

This book shows New Yorkers how the 1990 Charter provides additional access points for citizen participation. The council districts are smaller and, therefore, more representative of communities and of the people who reside in them. Equal opportunity and affirmative-action programs have been instituted. Community boards are forums for citizen participation and conduits for citizen complaints. The borough presidents and the council president receive complaints and look for patterns of problems. Community board, borough board, City Planning Commission and City Council hearings are open for public testimony. City agencies such as the Department for the Aging and the Consumer Affairs Department have citizen advisory councils.

Voter participation is being encouraged and facilitated. Public campaign financing has been instituted. Conflict-of-interest provisions have been codified and clarified.

And the city government is open to public scrutiny. Transcripts of meetings and public hearings are available. The city's books are examined by outside auditors. Management reports, statements of need and financial reports are submitted to the council, borough and community boards.

Service delivery is administratively decentralized so the needs of the local community can be more closely heeded.

All of this can mean a more open, responsive city. But city government will only be as responsive as an aware citizenry causes it to be. We hope this book gives you a better understanding of how New York City's government works and what you can do to make it responsive to your needs.

The League of Women Voters is a nonpartisan organization whose purpose is to promote informed and active citizen participation in government. It neither supports nor opposes candidates or political parties. Membership is open to all women and men who subscribe to its purpose.

The League is supported by membership dues and contributions from public-spirited individuals, businesses and organizations.

It maintains a Telephone Information Service weekdays from 10 a.m. to 4 p.m., Saturday from 10 a.m. to 1 p.m. Call (212) 674-8484.

The New York City League also publishes many citizen and voter information guides, including *They Represent You*, an annual compilation of the city, state and federal legislators who represent New York City. For a list of League publications, write to the League of Women Voters of the City of New York, 817 Broadway, New York, New York 10003-4760.